MORE GHOSTS IN THE VALLEY

Lynda Elizabeth Jeffrey

ISBN: 978-0-578-06814-5

Rowe Publishing
Washington, D.C.

Printed in the United States of America

Cover photographer: Linda Richters
Cover designer: Jennifer Rogers

To my father
who taught me that ghosts are a delicious terror
when you are holding someone's hand

AKTJ

To my loved ones—on both sides

LEJ

ALSO BY ADI-KENT THOMAS JEFFREY

The Bermuda Triangle
Triangle of Terror
They Dared the Devil's Triangle
Parallel Universe
Ghosts in the Valley
Haunted Village and Valley
Across Our Land From Ghost to Ghost
Ghosts of the Revolution
Witches and Wizards
They Dared Niagara

MORE GHOSTS IN THE VALLEY

MORE TRUE HAUNTINGS
IN THE DELAWARE VALLEY

Adi-Kent Thomas Jeffrey
Revised and Edited by Lynda Elizabeth Jeffrey

There is an atmosphere surrounding the vale (*valley*)
which often leaves an indelible impress upon the
spirits of the wayfarer; the highways and byways
in either direction seem to lead to shadowy glades,
wooded hills, misty river banks and forsaken dwellings.
Unlike many other localities, it possesses a certain mystery
which promises to excite emotion and unsettle the senses.
It is a destination worthy of notice.

*

REMINISCENSES OF BUCKS COUNTY
1883

CONTENTS

FOREWORD

My favorite state in the United States has always been Pennsylvania. In my childhood and early career I spent hundreds and hundreds of special hours there visiting with relatives and friends, specifically in the Lehigh Valley area. I am also very familiar with the Delaware Valley area, and New Hope has always had an enchanting and theatrical magic about it.

In all three of Adi-Kent Thomas Jeffrey's books (*Ghosts in the Valley*, *More Ghosts in the Valley*, and *Haunted Village and Valley*), she relates many fascinating incidents that allegedly occurred in this rich, colorful and historic area. Incidents that were recounted to her by scores of individuals. Rather than interpreting these experiences as encounters with dead "spirits," I prefer to call such encounters some kind of "ethereal communication." If you read between the lines, you'll understand that Adi also believed that "ghosts" were not actually spirits returning from the dead, but rather a manifestation of unconscious energy or force. I think this is a very important outlook to consider.

It's interesting that historically there has always been a remarkable surge of fascination with supernatural phenomena (the kinds of experiences that Adi embraces in her writings) during times in society when there has been difficulty, trouble, fear, and concern on a mass scale. In a sense, these anecdotes enable one to experience a relief. In my opinion, these newly revised editions of Adi-Kent Thomas Jeffrey's writings could not have been timed more appropriately.

I have a prediction to make for you, my dear reader, and that is that you will find the stories in this book to be more haunting than you ever expected. Each time you put down the book, the experiences you've just read will echo within you. You'll feel as if you are reliving them over and over again.

Adi-Kent Thomas Jeffrey knew how to bring chills to the spine and challenges to probing thought. And, the real beauty of this collection is that the stories are timeless. Enjoy!

The Amazing Kreskin
2011

PREFACE

"Adi-Kent Thomas Jeffrey, the Bucks County chronicler of ghosts, is at it again! It's good fun to find the lovely old homes and shadowy hills peopled with folk of the netherworld who love this area so much that they cannot leave. As for Mrs. Jeffrey, we devotedly hope that she will continue seeking them out." (*F.K. Brown, book critic for the Delaware Valley Advance.*)

Indeed, there was nothing that could stop my mother from chasing ghosts! After the highly acclaimed success of her book, *Ghosts in the Valley* (published in 1971), she pursued her role of "Supernatural Sleuth" with even more passion as she continued to seek out the mysterious, the inexplicable and the extraordinary. On any day of the week, you might see my mom zooming along the highways and byways of the Bucks County area in "Buttercup," our bright yellow Pontiac with stylish tail fins, as she headed for a haunted house, or an afternoon of "table-tilting" or perhaps an evening séance.

There's no doubt that the many years my mother served as a newspaper reporter helped to make her a top-notch investigator. She had an insatiable curiosity, a fearless spirit, a strong sense of intuition, a detective's probing mind, plus eyes and ears that were attuned to detail. Add those qualities to her natural graciousness, elegance and charm and you can bet that my mother was a psychic investigator like none other.

Were there more ghosts, troubled spirits and unseen visitors lurking along the dark side of the Delaware? Of course! As my mother used to say… "the possibilities of the Unseen World are endless!" During the time period from 1971-1973, she concentrated her efforts on gathering more real-life paranormal incidents, fascinating legends, and personal accounts of ghostly happenings and compiling them into a second volume of stories aptly named *More Ghosts in the Valley*. Needless to say, this new collection of spooky stories proved to be as popular as the first one.

Many decades have elapsed since both of these ghost books were originally published. There have been numerous printings of both volumes since the books first came out in the early '70s. *Ghosts in the Valley* has been printed ten times. This current edition marks the eighth printing for *More Ghosts in the Valley*. Truly, these are classic ghost stories that have never ceased to delight one generation of readers after another.

Yes, time marches on and, although the stories contained in both collections remain as alluring and fascinating as ever, I felt that it was time to give the books a new look. I think my mother would be pleased to know that her beloved ghosts are experiencing a surge of renewed energy. In my opinion, the graphic images and photographs give added enhancement to what the ghosts are trying to say. But I want to make it clear that the images are included only to enhance the reader's imagination. They are not being passed off as pictures of real ghosts! Readers will also notice that several of the stories are accompanied by beautifully drawn illustrations which are attributed to the Bucks County artist, Rochelle Boonshaft. My mother and my "Aunt Rochelle," as I affectionately used to call her, were life long friends. The two of them worked together as a successful writer/artist team. Their collaborated efforts appeared frequently in the local magazines *Bucks County Life* and *Panorama*. My sincere appreciation goes to Ann Madden and Peter Boonshaft for allowing me to include their mother's artwork, not only in this book, but in the other two ghost trilogy books as well.

Longtime fans of Adi-Kent Thomas Jeffrey will be happy to know that the text of *More Ghosts in the Valley* remains unchanged. The stories are exactly as my mother wrote them when she hammered out the words on her Smith-Corona typewriter. Obviously some of the references seem terribly outdated. You have to be of a certain age to remember such things as… clothespins, spinning tops, Mexican jumping beans, glass Coca-Cola bottles, and calico-printed housedresses, but I think these old-fashioned terms add a certain flavor and charm to the stories and it's my guess that most readers will find them amusing.

To old readers and new readers alike, I hope you will enjoy the "delicious terror" that awaits you within these pages. This is a timeless collection of fascinating, thought-provoking stories. *More Ghosts in the Valley* offers proof that there's more to life than meets the eye.

Lynda Elizabeth Jeffrey
2011

A ghost is both a clue and an invitation
to a world beyond our own limited reality,
an offer to broaden our awareness to encompass
everything and anything that might be possible.
And who can ignore that kind of challenge?

*

Antoinette May

INTRODUCTION

The dark belongs to the Delaware. Anyone who has lived along its shores can tell you that. In spite of extensive modernization; industrial development; super highways and housing expansion, there are still unlit stretches of forests and glens; dismal swamps; shadow-hidden streams and night-cooled gullies. There are covered bridges; narrow city alleyways and many, many old houses in city and country—all of which carry the mark of the dark hand of Fate.

I have lived in Bucks County on the Delaware for over twenty years and have been infatuated with its storied past every moment of those years. I am not the first. Many writers sang of it before. Great ones. Walt Whitman; James Fenimore Cooper; John Greenleaf Whittier; and the maestro of horror and the morbid, Edgar Allen Poe—all were here.

And before them, others were passing through, leaving their impress. The Lenni-Lenape Indians; William Penn and the early Quaker immigrants; pioneer settlers; explorers; adventurers; pirates; murderers; outlaws; spies; and more ghosts than imaginable. There were also history-makers like Washington, Lafayette, John Adams, James Monroe and Ulysses S. Grant. There were the brave and courageous patriots who fought and bled for our country's freedom; the rugged hard-working laborers; the bold entrepreneurs; the gifted artisans; the stalwart women and the high-spirited children. In short, all of America was represented here.

With such a rich historical and cultural heritage, is it any wonder that so many restless spirits still hover over the Delaware Valley region? As I have discovered during my last two years of investigating paranormal phenomena, there have always been—and always will be—dark-sided deeds, eerie events and ghosts galore stirring from one corner of this valley to another!

I hope you will enjoy this new collection of baffling, exhilarating, absorbing and astonishing stories… *true* stories… and that upon closing this book you'll find yourself pondering, with even greater curiosity, the Unknown mysteries of life. Nothing would please me more.

Adi-Kent Thomas Jeffrey
1973

MIDNIGHT MESSAGE

Dr. S. Weir Mitchell dimmed the gas light in his study and started for his bed chamber. The hall clock struck twelve as he dragged by.

It had been a long day, one patient after another. At his age, this was not an easy day. He had just finished a cup of warm milk and was headed for the inviting depths of his feather bed. It was a restless midnight, he thought. The wind was blowing a December blizzard along Philadelphia's streets outside. He could hear the snapping of icy flakes against the windows.

Dr. Mitchell yawned as he reached for the shadowy banister. His hand stayed in mid-air. The front door bell had rung so violently, he was frozen to a standstill.

Who on earth could be at his door at this hour in such weather?

He held the lapels of his smoking jacket across his chest as a cracking wind swept against him. In the open doorway stood a young girl. She was no more than ten years old. She stood thin as a willow branch in the pounding snow, with nothing on but a cotton dress and a ragged red shawl about her shoulders and over her head. Her eyes were black as coal tar in her white face.

"Are you the doctor?" Her voice was as cold and flat as the stone step on which she stood.

"Yes," admitted Dr. Mitchell but hastened to add that he had not gone out on night calls for some time.

The child looked steadily at him as she spoke. It was as if he had said nothing at all. "Will you please come with me? My mother is very sick. She needs a doctor badly."

Dr. Mitchell sighed and shook his head. "Come on in," he directed and shut the door after her. "My child, do you not have a regular physician to call upon?"

The young girl ran her fingers along the edge of her red shawl. She stared straight into the doctor's face with large luminous eyes. "She needs you," she replied evenly. "Won't you please come?"

Dr. Mitchell straightened and sighed again. "Very well. Wait here while I get dressed. I was about to retire you see, but—"

He said no more. The girl's gaze struck his heart like a tiny knife.

"I'll be down in a moment," he said as he started up the stairs.

When he came down, the child was still standing where he had left her. She hadn't seemed to move the clutch of her hands on the shawl or the straight-ahead gaze of her eyes.

The moment Dr. Mitchell opened the front door, the young girl was ahead of him, gliding down the stairs and along the streets. The snow swirled around her red-shawled head and shoulders. Never did she pause or bend against the wind or sweep the icy wet from her face. The snow scarcely seemed to touch her. The doctor bent his head and squinted against the driving force as he followed down one long block after another.

Here they turned, there they ducked, until he found that they were climbing a flight of steps to an old rooming house. The girl's shawl fluttered one last moment, then they were inside a dimly-lit hallway. A gas jet sputtered on the wall in the draught. Pieces of trash and garbage stirred in the hall corners. The odor was near nauseating.

The doctor shook bits of ice from his overcoat.

"Well, young lady, where do we go from here?" The doctor stifled a cough from the reeking air.

The child answered nothing. Still hugging her shawl, she mounted the steps. Up one flight, then another. On the third floor she led him to a back room and opened the door. The room flooded him with a feeling of cold and neglect. In the faint light from a candle on a long table, Dr. Mitchell saw the form of a woman in the bed. She lay still.

Her breathing was labored.

He swiftly opened his bag and leaned over the pale face. He listened to her heart; felt her pulse.

"Why, I know you," he said as he stood upright and turned to the girl still standing in the doorway. "Your mother used to work for me. Years before you were born, I daresay."

The child looked back at him, staring into his eyes. She said nothing.

"Your mother is in delirium. Pneumonia. I must contact the hospital for aid immediately. Is there a telephone in the building?" The doctor flicked an anxious glance at the dying woman; then back to her child.

"Not in this house, but I can show you where there is a telephone next door." Quickly the girl glided before him down the dreary steps, out into the wild night. In the building next door, the doctor placed his call.

It was the longest night the doctor had ever experienced. The waiting in the dark room; the listening to the woman's hard breathing. Then the arrival of help from the hospital. As he worked he knew nothing but that he was fighting to save a woman's life.

When the first glimmer of dawn filtered into the room, the doctor strained to see his patient's face. She opened her eyes. Her breathing came free and easy. The doctor wiped his forehead with his handkerchief. She would be all right. He had won his battle.

The woman turned slightly. Her lips parted with surprise. "Dr. Mitchell! How did you get here?"

"Don't you know?" asked the doctor with a soft smile. "Your daughter fetched me. Through a blinding snow storm that would have discouraged the stoutest of men, she came and found me and brought me here."

The woman struggled and raised herself up on one elbow. Her brows were knit in puzzlement. Dr. Mitchell was packing his instruments into his black bag.

"By the way," he asked, "where is your daughter? I haven't seen her since she led me to a telephone next door and back here again."

The woman ran her fingers through her hair, tossing her head slightly. "I just don't understand what you are talking about, Dr.

Mitchell."

"I am speaking of your very intelligent and appealing daughter who fetched me from my home last midnight. I don't usually make night calls anymore but her eyes were so imploring and her manner so insistent, she persuaded me!" The doctor peered out the open doorway into the hall. "I don't see her, but will you be sure to give her my warmest regards? She may come to see me anytime."

The woman's face, lifted up towards his was whiter than ever. Tears trickled down her cheeks.

"My daughter is dead, doctor. She died a month ago." There was only silence in the room. Dr. Mitchell looked down at his patient, unbelieving. "If you look in the cupboard," she went on, "you will find her clothes still hanging right where she left them."

With stunned movements the doctor parted the rotting doors of the room's cupboard and stared in. Hanging on the hook was a thin cotton dress and a red shawl, which were utterly dry to the doctor's touch. These garments could not possibly have been out in the icy night.

Dr. Mitchell returned home that morning. But he was never again quite the same man he had been before. An experience had occurred that he was never able to forget.

So goes the story of what happened one winter night in the late 1800s to the foremost neurologist of America.

Dr. Silas Weir Mitchell was not only an eminent physician, he was President of the Association of American Physicians; President of the American Neurologist Association; a holder of many university degrees; as well as a novelist of great reputation.

Not a man of illusionary visions, he was first and foremost a scientist. But the incident with the child in the red shawl haunted him until the day he died. He spoke of it often. He was never able to explain it.

DIRE DOINGS IN DYERSTOWN

A few miles north of Doylestown proper in Bucks County, Pennsylvania, there is a hamlet that has proudly retained its original identity in spite of plans, zones, discussions and all the what-have-you's of the modern day.

The place is Dyerstown, settled in 1714 by one John Dyer. The rural winding road and past century charm that once pervaded the scene hovers yet in the old stone homes, great-boughed trees and singing streams.

The grist mill, built by John Dyer, still stands and serves as a noble inn to the hungry traveler. Operated by Ruth and Charles Kiker, it is called The Water Wheel Inn. And it boasts a rarity—just about the largest wooden cog wheel still in its original position.

It is also reputed to have another rarity—a ghost.

Like many ghosts, this fellow has prestige. (And why not? Guests at the inn in the past included Dorothy Parker, Katherine Anne Porter, James Cagney and many a visiting artist, writer or actor.) But the personality that this haunter relates to is of great historical importance—The General Marquis de Lafayette.

It seems that in August of 1777, when Lafayette and his forces were encamped down in the valley of Pine Run, the French General dined at John Dyer's Inn. Ever since, as the story goes, on the anniversary of his visit, the romantic Frenchman returns, seeking the old cordiality of wine and bread.

Mr. and Mrs. John Corcoran, owners of The Water Wheel Inn, in past years have gone out of their way to be hosts to this restless soul. On the August anniversary, they set apart a table for the "guest" from the Other World complete with burning candles, a French baguette and a glass of Bordeaux wine.

But that's not the only intriguing "doings" going on at the old inn. I learned recently of a fascinating incident that occurred to one of the employees of the establishment. He was sitting alone by a front window late at night reviewing some business matters, when he was nearly startled out of his chair by a low voice, calling through the room!

The man stopped what he was doing and listened, spellbound!

Again it called. "John! John!"

The man swallowed, thought a second, then decided to speak out. "My name is not John," he announced. Then he gave out to the semi-darkness his own name.

There was a moment of complete silence followed by a quick

breath and an, "Oh!"

Nothing more. The man didn't need anymore. He closed up the inn and went home.

I sat at that same table, also quite alone, listening attentively for any kind of voice or utterance. There was no sound, to my regret. Perhaps, the "seeker" has learned that John Dyer, the original owner, is truly not there.

Of course, there is a John Dyer in Bucks County today of that family—as there has been every generation since the first settler.

I wondered to myself... is the ghost trying to beckon him?

Then, I mused, there is of course, John Corcoran, the well known radio newscaster, who gave so much of his good cheer and liberal hospitality to the inn. Perhaps, he is the one being summoned!

Well, I left the heritage-rich, old-time hostelry and went next door to visit another Dyerstown "haunting ground"—the home of Woody Best, where supernatural talk and tea go together as naturally and warmly as honey and hot biscuits.

One may not think of the supernatural in terms of being "warm." With Woody, it is. She is a friend by nature. Friend with a capital "F." Everything connected with her reflects this warmth. Even the strange experience she related to me, seemed not cold and eerie but sweet and loving.

It all happened a few years ago when Woody Best was the new mistress of the old Dyerstown house that once served as the village post office. In the middle of the night, she heard a knocking on a door downstairs. She donned slippers and robe and padded down the steps to the front room where several doors exist. She listened a moment and realized the knocking was not on any of these doors, but on the wall at the far end of the room which is used by the Bests as a den. Though covered now as a wall, the front part of that room when a post office, did have a door there.

"You can't come in that way," called Mrs. Best. "There is no door for me to open. But come around to the side. I'll open that one for you." Woody crossed over to the other side of the house and unlocked the door, opening it wide. There was nothing but a cool, night wind.

Woody looked at me with honest blue eyes that seemed at peace with all the world.

"I know on the surface of things, that sounds so foolish. For me to open up an outside door in the middle of the night to a strange knocking. But then, to me, somehow it was not strange. I felt it was a friendly person who wanted to come into our home. I wasn't a bit afraid."

Although the knocking ceased after she opened the door, Woody waited, scanning the quiet outdoors. Nothing happened. She said softly, "It's all right, I don't mind. It was no trouble."

She closed and locked the side door and went back upstairs to bed.

The same incident occurred not too many nights after that. This time the knocking was on the front door.

"I opened it up again and invited my ghostly visitant in, but nothing happened. Or, perhaps, I just think nothing happened. The spirit may very well have come in—and may still be here. Sometimes I feel that it is."

My hostess lit a cigarette slowly, then sighed, "Whatever is going on, you know, I don't mind it at all. I'm never afraid of his presence. If it were an ordinary knocking on the outside door in the middle of the night, I'm sure my heart would leap into my throat. But, I have never felt it was human. I seem always to sense it's some gentle spirit form, who simply wants to visit me. He can come all he wants, you know. I shall never be afraid of him."

I am sure she never will be. Woody Best, like Dyerstown's mellow mill next door, and the peaceful road outside and the wild-growing

Queen Anne's Lace flocking the meadows here and there, radiates warmth and welcome to all the world.

HOUSE WITH A CURSE

There has never been an estate more beautiful than a historic mansion near a cool-eyed pond in Milford, Delaware. When a man, whom we shall call "Harvey," and his wife took over the homestead some years ago, they removed the fabulously beautiful woodwork and sold it, redecorating the house to their own taste.

It would seem this altering touch set off a chain of unusual circumstances that many attribute to the occult.

In the early days of the estate's centuries-old life, the owners had a Negro servant, a beautiful girl, whom we shall call "Esther."

Many a man about the local plantations kept a hungry eye on the lovely young girl as she moved through the fields, her curved hips swaying freely from side to side under loosely gathered calico skirts. Her dark eyes and gleaming smile were tantalizingly hidden behind the screen of a large sunbonnet. It was her favorite practice to turn slowly when she heard the footsteps of a man and with a tilt of her head, peer upwards towards him.

It wasn't long before someone decided to accept the inviting eyes. In the middle of the night, Esther's door slowly opened and a man slipped into her room. The moonlight caught his eager features for a brief moment.

"Who are you?" cried out the girl. She sat up with a patchwork quilt held close just under her naked breasts. It was the man she hoped it was.

"So, you are not so unfeeling. You do have the passions of the common man, even for such a lowly one as I. Well, you shall not touch me, however much you desire to do so, for I am unapproachable! I am a Voodoo witch! I now place a curse on you and this house and all who dare to defy my power or defile my person!"

The man snickered. She could hear his heavy breathing as he came nearer and nearer in the darkness.

In the next moment she felt herself thrown backwards and the awful weight of the man thrown across her. She plunged her fingers into his eyes and face. She would not scream. That would be useless. He rolled over, groaning, and she bolted out of the bed. The door was locked and the key gone. She flew to the window, throwing the casement open wide. She knew the Negro man whose room was just overhead would hear her call, but there was no time for a word. The man was at her side, pressing her powerfully with his huge arms. Not towards him, but away! She struggled with teeth gritted but it was useless. She felt herself slipping farther and farther out the window until there was no pressure left but only freedom and a headlong falling towards the ground below.

No one inquired too thoroughly what had happened to Esther. Or why she had thrown herself from her bedroom window. She was quietly buried without fuss in her long calico skirts and her yellow sunbonnet.

But was the estate ever the same without Esther? Did it feel the malevolence of her curse? Some say it did. The house was once swept by fire. Another time, a whole row of poplars was struck down by a storm as though some giant hand had dealt a crushing blow at the lot of them. Mrs. Harvey herself was plagued by illness and nearly died of a severe heart attack while living in the house.

One day the gardener of the estate, while digging the ground to plant a new flower bed, unearthed a group of old hand-blown bottles. They had been buried with the open neck down. When examined by a glass expert they were identified as old Voodoo bottles. The custom was to encase magic potions with evil purposes into the bottles, then bury them with the open neck down. The belief of the witch doctors was that as the contents seeped into the ground, the curse on the property would be affected.

Accidentally, the man who decided to store the historic bottles away in a vault broke them. He, too, suffered a heart attack.

Mrs. Harvey began fervently to wish she'd never laid eyes on the old historic place!

This wish became more ardent following one eventful night. After crawling into bed, she was lying alone in the darkness watching the moon's rays pour in through the open window of the little upstairs bedroom. All of a sudden she heard the door click open. She looked up to see the form of a young girl glide quietly across the room. She was dressed in long calico skirts which swayed as she walked like a sinuous snake. On her head was a large sunbonnet. When the figure reached the window, it leaned slowly over the ledge—then vanished. There was nothing left to Mrs. Harvey's vision but a blanket of moonlight stretched across the sill.

I don't know when the Harveys moved away from the great house, but I venture to say, it wasn't too long after Esther paid her final call.

As for the Voodoo curse, it seems to have vanished with her.

"DESIRE UNDER THE ELMS"... AND GHOSTS?

When the renowned actor of the 1800s, James O'Neill, picked up a lagging mortgage from a fellow theatrical personage, did he also buy a ghost?

O'Neill never knew it, if he did. He had displayed and portrayed the stoutest courage in his long-running performances as the sword-wielding "Count of Monte Cristo," but would he have been as fearless in his newly-acquired house in Rock Mills, New Jersey?

The actor never lived in the old Revolutionary structure, so he never met its ghosts. He just kept an eye on his property, sweeping into the tiny village from time to time to check out the place and keep it in shape. His visits were memorable because he was a memorable person. With a skill for dramatics, he kept the attention of every villager, as he recounted tale after tale, in the post office or the village store.

In the winter and spring of 1909-1910, the famous actor's twenty-one-year-old son, Eugene, arrived in Rock Mills and took over the cottage down by the old mill creek. With "Gene" was his good friend,

George Bellows, an artist already making a name for his "realistic, unselfconscious style," as some called it.

The two youths spent easy-going leisurely months, each doing "his own thing." What their interests were, was not much a topic of conversation around the crossroads settlement—chiefly because it wasn't much the conversation from the boys themselves. When pressed, Gene O'Neill would allow that he liked to "try a little writing —but I wouldn't tell anybody!" And George—well, he didn't have to say anything to anyone. You could always see him here and there, in the snow; in the middle of the road; or sitting by the old mill creek with paintbrush in hand splashing bright colors across a canvas.

When the two young men pulled up typewriter and easel at the end of that summer of 1910, they left behind an unusual heritage. A different one from the famous skills of each. Nothing to do with the remarkable prizefighter scenes of George Bellows or the sensitive and symbolic themes of Eugene O'Neill's *Anna Christie*, or *The Hairy Ape*, or the unforgettable *Desire Under the Elms*. These were all gifts for the world yet to come.

They left a memory; an air of forgotten time of life; an atmosphere of haunting recollections to which they each unconsciously contributed.

That atmosphere may have touched their sensitivities in ways they never mentioned and about which we can never know. But atmosphere there was in that old Revolutionary house with its wide-plank flooring; deep plastered stone walls; centuries-old hearths and a well-deep storage of memories. A resident of that place many years ago, known only as "Old Man Hawkins," was an integral part of that musty air. Often his bent form was seen wandering among the blackberry canes and stooping to drink from Rock Brook's bubbling falls (which George Bellows loved equally as much and immortalized on canvas).

Old Hawkins felt the creaky Revolutionary house was filled with spirits from the past. One in particular he dubbed "Richard." Richard was present frequently. He made himself known, claimed the old man, by a footfall on a floor board; or by rapping on the old walls; or by pulling the bedcovers off one in the middle of the night.

Many a time, neighbors reported seeing Old Hawkins stop abruptly what he was doing, look upwards into space and then with a firm nod, announce, "Oh, I know, Richard. I know. Just a moment, I'll be there." With that, the old man would open up his front door and disappear into the dark.

Nobody ever learned who Richard was. No one really knew who "Old Man Hawkins" was. Today, none of the past is known of the passing travelers. The dimly-lit rooms of the old eighteenth century structure have vanished, along with their thick walls and the back porch laden with shading vines that O'Neill and Bellows liked so well. Gone, too, are the blackberry bushes, the cedars, and even, the old sturdy elms. Also, the name "Rock Mills" has faded into obscurity. The name was changed early in this century to "Zion." A double name became too complicated for the post office. Since the mills had long since been gone and little lingered of the old days, save the Mount Zion Church "up the road a piece," the name "Zion" became the only sensible name left to give the place. So, it is today. The name; the church; the glimmer of falls by the bridge; and even some stray goldenrod still can be seen to recall the past. And, of course, to the psychically sensitive, old and restless ghosts haunt the ground and the air.

Some say the spirits are those of dead Hessians who hid out in the hills after the defeat at Trenton. Some say they are the dark-dwelling "Richard." Others suggest Eugene O'Neill and George Bellows return on moonlit nights. Perhaps all of them roam these midland New Jersey hills.

Why else would this hill region have been labeled, "Spook Mountains"?

Ghosts That Go To College

When one happens upon the Eastern Baptist College in St. Davids, Pennsylvania, it doesn't require much imagination to see that the place was once one of the most fabulous palatial dwellings in all of America.

Walk past the lake, up the winding drives, gaze at the tile roof, the stained glass windows and thick ivy-shrouded walls. Already, you have shared the beauty that was always a part of "Walmarthon" since its builder and owner, Charles Walton, had it constructed in the early 1900s.

The house is a wealth of beautiful materials. The rough tile one sees everywhere was imported from Italy, as were the marble columns and mantels scattered magnificently throughout the house—from the Octagonal Room where Mrs. Walton served tea to the "Ladies' Retiring Room" just on one's right as the house is entered. The finished colorful tiles one sees all about were the creations of Henry Mercer of the renowned Doylestown Mercer Tile Company. Most of the woodwork is natural mahogany. The painted ceiling that still reaches down to the appraising eye with majesty was done by the famous mural painter of the last century, Albert Herter (father of Christian Herter, former Secretary of State under Eisenhower).

The grounds to the estate carry a history with them. They were once the hunting and camping sites of the Lenni-Lenape Indians.

Eagle Road was an old Indian trail. Arrowheads have been discovered frequently over the years.

So much for the rich historical and cultural heritage that shapes the present campus of Eastern Baptist College.

Is there also a ghost in that legacy?

If the manifold tales that have been circulating the halls and rooms of the institution for the past decade are to be believed, there is. The haunting spirit of a young child about six or seven years old.

I talked to several students and some graduates from the college. They all agreed that the ghost story was one of the first bits of "knowledge" passed on to them in their Freshman year.

Several professors with whom I spoke were familiar with the tale, and in some cases, had what one might call a first-hand experience with it. But the Halls of Learning, being the erudite and respectable institutions that they are, are reluctant to accept a ghost.

So, without any official sanction from the college or any of its personnel, I merely pass on what I heard.

The little girl seems to be a most "spirited" one, if you'll pardon

the expression. She likes the dormitory halls and flits up and down them, creating cold draughts of air as she passes. Once when a group of some twenty female students had gathered for a séance, the girls declared they felt her presence come into the room and the temperature noticeably drop to such a degree they shivered. Other students declare that they have heard screams after midnight issuing from the upper closed-off portions of the "tower room."

A recent graduate informed me that one of the security officers confided in her about a weird experience he had every night.

One of his responsibilities was to punch the time clock on the fourth floor of the main building. On the midnight hour, the ghost would lift the key and chain for him! He distinctly felt the cold whirl around him as the strange operation took place in front of his unbelieving eyes.

But the most appealing stories are those in which someone reported that, upon hearing a knock on the door and opening it, a young child came in, danced around the room and departed. In one case, it was recounted as being several children.

What can be behind the apparitions, if anything is? The only solid fact I could unearth was that Charles Walton, owner of Walmarthon, had a daughter, Suzanne, who died at the age of seven.

The students think she likes their presence in her old home and wants to be with them to play or to share or to help.

A neighbor of mine, Barbara Burger, of Warminster, Pennsylvania, adds an interesting appendix to the reputed ghostly capers of Eastern Baptist Seminary at Lancaster Avenue and City Line. Some students she knows once told her about the appearance, from time to time, of a ghost foot. No other body part manifests itself but this one strange phantom foot! A large white blob with freakishly long toes that is clearly the terminal end of some leg!

What explanation for that? Well, a rather ghoulish one, if one lets his imagination supply a solution. The seminary is reputed to have been a "hang-out" at one time for some gangsters. More thugs than one have reduced a body to separate members and buried them.

May no one ever go "digging" around the halls and grounds of Eastern Baptist Seminary!

"One More Time…"

As the old time vaudeville players called out when their act was favorably received… "One more time!" so it would seem the ghosts of an old house on Aquetong Road in New Hope, Pennsylvania, wish frequently to "go into their act" and do it again.

The house created its first known stir when the John Loepers occupied it some years ago. (The ghostly goings-on they experienced appear in my book, *Ghosts in the Valley*, under the title, "The House with Things that Go Bump.")

But just because the Loepers moved away, one mustn't construe that the invisible inhabitants did also. Far from it!

A family that followed on the heels of the Loepers found life every bit as fantastic in that old house.

For one thing, the cushions on the sofa and chairs in the living room refused to stay put. On a particularly well-recalled occasion, the lady of the house was sitting on the sofa, sewing, when the back cushion on a large armchair opposite her suddenly pitched forward and tumbled towards her on to the floor.

Another time, the husband went downstairs in the night to check a noise and felt the eerie sensation of something in front of the fireplace brushing against his legs. There were no indoor plants near the fireplace and no pets in the home.

The fireplace seems to serve as a focal point for one of the strangest incidents that occurs and reoccurs in that house. Somehow, the shoes of the man of the house end up in the fireplace!

The very last day as this family was moving out, the husband took a final look around the house and noticed a weird thing. The stuffing

and padding he had rammed up into the chimney flue to keep out drafts a long time before, was all down and filling the hearth. An amazing thing since the packing material had been squeezed in air-tight and it had held there for a long time. But the part that startled him the most was the fact that, resting on top of the wadding and rags, was an old pair of his shoes which he had discarded and left upstairs!

This same incident happened again with the next tenants to move into the old house, Peter and Natachia Dodd. One day, the couple looked into the fireplace to find Mr. Dodd's shoes resting peacefully inside the hearth.

But so many other things occurred to the Dodds that were far from peaceful. Natachia recalls them well to this day, though she has long since moved away from Aquetong Road.

The first thing the new owner of the house became conscious of was a phenomenon the two previous residents had complained of—noises from the third floor. Both former tenants had mentioned hearing inexplicable sounds from the top floor. The Loepers described heavy footsteps. The new owners complained of harsh scraping sounds like chairs being dragged across the bare floor.

When Natachia Dodd began to hear the sounds, she and her husband felt sure there must be tree limbs raking the walls or roof of the house on windy days. But investigation proved that nothing was touching the house at all. Then they thought it might be possible that some squirrel or raccoon had made a home in the upper reaches of the place, but they could find no trace of any such intrusion.

"Finally, I decided there was nothing to do but accept the peculiarity and live with it, whether it was old squeaking boards or howling wind through open knot holes. I was an artist and I didn't have time to think about anything other than setting up my studio and getting to work."

The third floor seemed the only available spot for the workshop, so up went her easel, paint pots and canvases and in no time at all, Natachia was producing.

But what was she producing? It amazed her when she finally sat back and took stock. The most macabre kind of subject matter. Symbolic landscapes that suggested death, destruction, the end of the world. Broken hourglasses, skeletons, and a black raven on a barren tree limb. Natachia bit on the end of a paintbrush. She had never painted like that before. What was happening to her?

She decided to take the situation in hand one day. She deliberately painted the most innocent portrayal possible... a depiction of

Donald Duck. It would please her little daughter and it would bring a note of freshness to the bleak world she'd been immersed in without even realizing it.

At the end of the day, Natachia stood back and glanced over the cartoon portrait. The bright yellow beak; the vivid blue sailor shirt and cap; the happy eyes all looked back at her with joy. She sprayed a fixative over the water color and left it to dry. Before retiring that night she took another look. Dried and finished, it pleased her as much as it had when she had just completed it. She went to bed feeling more uplifted than she had in a long time.

The next morning came the shock.

When Natachia went into her studio, she stopped cold at the threshold. The Donald Duck portrait rested on the easel right where she'd left it, but now tears trickled downwards from the animal's eyes! The rest of the painting was smeared and streaked with scrawled letters that formed an indistinguishable word.

Natachia was stunned! How was it possible that anyone could have done this? How could anyone have gotten into the house? And, even if they had, how could they have tampered with her painting after it had been coated with such a heavy layer of protective varnish? It was impossible! Yet it had happened.

But even more inexplicable things were to happen in the Dodd household.

Natachia's sister, Carolyn Lockwood, and her husband, stayed for a short time with the Dodds while locating a new home for themselves. During their stay, the in-laws occupied the third floor. One night, Carolyn, only half asleep in bed, became aware that someone had come into the bedroom. She opened her eyes and saw a man standing close by her. He was dressed in a velvet jacket, satin breeches and a powdered wig. His white face looked worn and weary. He held one hand over his heart as though it troubled him. Then before Carolyn could move, he vanished.

Natachia listened attentively to her sister's story the next day. In fact, she mulled over the incident repeatedly for some time to come. Not long after the Lockwoods' departure one quiet day, Natachia Dodd decided to spend the morning catching up on the wash. She was on the third floor about to hang up the wet clothes in the narrow little hallway when a quick thought popped into her head.

Something more important than hanging up the wash was paramount in her mind at that moment. She dropped the clothespins back into her apron pocket, stepped away from the wicker laundry basket for a second and called out in a firm voice… "If somebody is here and my sister saw you, then give me a sign!"

With that, the pile of wet clothes in the basket at her feet flew upwards and scattered all over the hallway!

Natachia picked up the clothes in a near stunned state. She had no sooner filled the basket when—Zoom—upward flew the wash again! Once more, she patiently returned the items to their wicker container and once again, they scattered all around her!

At this point, Mrs. Dodd decided to call it quits. She went downstairs for a couple of hours to recover. Not until later, when she cautiously tried again, was she able to proceed with her routine laundry chores in a normal manner.

Today, Natachia and her husband have moved to a new house in another area of New Hope. But the memories of the old Aquetong house are never far out of mind.

Strange incidents have occurred where she is now living, too. Bolted doors are found open. Her dog growls and cowers for no apparent reason. Have some of the troubled spirits come with her? Checking with the family who followed the Loepers, I found that one strange thing has happened to them in their present home. The wife bought an antique child's wooden stocking stretcher to hang by the fireside for decorative effect. The next day she noted a wet patch on the hearth stones beneath it. When she touched the toe of the tiny wooden-shaped foot it felt damp to her fingers. She dried off the stocking frame and the moisture that had accumulated on the flagstone and forgot about it. The next day the wet spot was back! Several times this occurred with no apparent cause that she could determine. For the moment, though, the mysterious "dripping" has ceased and all is at peace in the new home.

For the time being, as far as I can determine, everything up at the old Aquetong house is quiet also. The ghosts, perhaps, are tired of their acts and are no longer willing to do them even "one more time."

Home for Haunters—Greenwich, New Jersey

Should you be wondering if the Delaware Valley has a preserved centuries-old village deserving of unusual historic recognition—rest assured it does. Greenwich, New Jersey.

The moment you drive into town, gliding serenely down Ye Greate Street with its heavily-limbed trees branching overhead and its perfectly-kept seventeenth and eighteenth century homes flanking the road, you feel as though you've gone back in time at least a hundred years. I know I did.

So, apparently, do the spirits of this village. They must be so convinced their era yet remains, they simply will not go off somewhere else and rest. They roam the byways, the waterways and a surprising number of local homes. One might even, by a little stretch of the psychic sense, refer to the whole area as a "Haunted Village."

Tale of a Pirate

One of the most famous haunted houses in Greenwich is an old brick home familiar to every resident in town.

The tale, told and retold about the house built in the eighteenth century, states that a pirate once lived there. He set sail on a long voyage after double-crossing his fellow buccaneers in a gold-sharing deal and didn't return for many years afterwards.

But, pirates have long memories, with strong vengeful hands. And when the schemer finally returned to his home, the old partners were waiting for him. They killed him and chained his body in the attic where he, himself, had tied many a prisoner in his youth. Now he is the eternal prisoner. His spirit stalks the old attic boards late at night and some past occupants, I was told, stated they heard the rattling of chains clanking above at the midnight hour.

THE INVISIBLE BUCCANEER

I found pirate lore is rampant in old Greenwich and its surrounding country side. Oldtimers will tell you how their parents and grandparents spoke of the many buccaneers who landed on the Jersey shores and buried their treasure there. Certainly their presence is historical fact, as newspapers of the day mentioned it. For example, the Philadelphia press wrote on June 1, 1699:

"There is arrived into this Government about sixty Pirates in a ship directly from Malligasco. They are part of Kidd's Gang... "

In the marshes around Bacons Neck, just outside Greenwich, are several small islands said to be the burying ground of many a chest of gleaming coins.

But the most intriguing tale tells the weird instance on Blackbeard's ship when crew members noticed from time to time in their midst, an unidentified man. Sometimes they'd spot him on deck—sometimes below. Never able to get to him to ask who he was, he

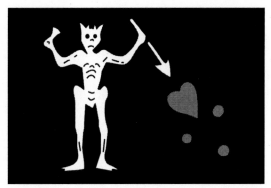

Blackbeard's flag featured a devil-horned skeleton.

always seemed to disappear to another part of the ship. Eventually, he vanished for good. Blackbeard's men always claimed after that voyage, that the devil had sailed with them.

BACONS NECK AND ITS NOISY GHOSTS

In an old frame house on a back road outside of Greenwich, in an area known as Bacons Neck, a variety of ghostly troublemakers roam the well-worn floor boards. At least they did when Lee and Carol

Richardson lived there a short time ago.

In spite of the many windows, one of the first things Carol and Lee noticed was that the house always seemed so dark inside—and oppressive. But maybe, says Carol, their real trouble began when they had to take the old stairs down in order to get their queen-sized bed up the steps. For days afterwards, the couple heard footsteps at night.

But that was just a starter. Things went wild after that. The radio volume would be turned up when no one was near it. The clothes dryer went on mysteriously. Lights went off and on. Several times the couple found themselves locked out of the house. Once they even found their child's door was locked from the inside while she was asleep.

On another occasion, Carol couldn't locate an old quilt she kept in the family room. Later, she found it jammed into the baby's bassinet stored in a corner of the attic.

Other signs of ghostly intruders are even more substantial, Carol tells you. At the top of the first landing is a room that has a sealed-off doorway. When a former owner enlarged the building, a door in the room was left in place but opened to nothing but a blank wall.

On several occasions when visitors stayed in that bedroom, they claimed they saw that old door open up and a figure come into the room. It was a little demure Quaker lady, complete with gray shawl and bonnet. She would step to the foot of the bed and stand silently there for several minutes before departing into the shadows.

"It's strange," says Carol, "but our daughter has said to us several times that she has seen some 'granny' come into her room at night. She wears a 'pretty cap on her head'."

Who is the apparition? Well, the house once belonged to the founding family of the Bacons, who were staunch Quakers and skilled mariners. Samuel Bacon settled in that area in the late 1600s.

Perhaps, the gentle little woman is one of his descendants.

Be that as it may, the Richardsons pulled up their shaking stakes from Bacons Neck and now reside in a bright and cheerful Victorian home on the other side of Greenwich.

GHOST FROM THE GAY NINETIES

The Richardsons love their newly-settled Victorian abode and are enjoying its quiet for a change. But on Ye Greate Street, in the heart of Greenwich, another family is enjoying their Victorian house, too. Including its disturbance!

Actually, no one could call the quiet and inoffensive lady, who comes calling in phantom fashion on the Root family, a disturbance. At least, the Roots do not. They have the feeling that this woman belongs there as much as they. They even wish, I suspect, that she would come to visit more often.

The ghostly caller at the Root's charming frame house is a fashionable young woman dressed in the style of the Gay Nineties era. Her dark hair is tossed high in a pompadour much like the "Gibson Girl" drawings so famous in the late 1800s.

She is always dressed in a black skirt pinched into a tight belt line with a fan-front bodice featuring a lavish ruffled trim. From her ears dangle delicate pendulum earrings.

"She is so flesh and blood," Winifred Root explained to me, "that the first time I saw her, I was startled that a stranger had gotten into our house. Then slowly, I began to realize she was of another time; another era.

"I had been sitting right here in this living room chair, facing the entrance hall and the foot of the stairs, when I happened to glance up and caught sight of this figure. Dressed in her black skirt with its tight-fitting waist, she was so distinct I thought a neighbor had come in. I could see clearly every feature of her face—her black eyes; dark hair; even the earrings that swung from her ears. I was so surprised, I couldn't speak—neither did she. She just leaned casually against the newel post at the foot of the stairs and gazed at me. The next thing I knew, she was gone!"

"Yes, you know," added Walter Root, "we have never believed this sort of thing or ever experienced anything like it. Yet, we should have been suspicious. We found the house and bought it, just like that, at a wonderful price!"

Has Mrs. Root seen the handsome woman since?

"Oh, my yes—at least a half dozen times. Once, I heard the cellar door that opens to the hallway click open. I was concerned, for I was alone in the house. I glanced up and saw our lady come through the basement doorway, enter the living room and walk towards the desk in the corner. Then she vanished.

"At other times, I have seen her standing in a doorway to one of the rooms, either upstairs or down, with her arms folded, just watching me."

Does Winifred Root have any idea who she is?

"Well, not long after I first saw her, I had a friend visiting and we decided to try a kind of ouija board method to see if we could contact her. We put letters of the alphabet in a circle around my dining room table, then we both put our fingers on the rim of a wine glass. The glass started moving very quickly and it spelled out the name, 'Nora.'

"In checking with local people, who knew former owners here, one of them told me there was someone once by the name of Nora who lived here. So I think there can be no doubt that Nora, whoever she is, comes back to this house that was hers here on earth."

"Has anyone else seen the ghost lady?"

"Yes, my daughter Barbara has, on several occasions. Though, like me, she may not see her for months and months, then, all of a sudden, she'll see her several times in a row. Maybe on the stair landing, maybe in the attic. Sometimes the lady will just be standing by Barbara's dresser. Just this past July, after arriving home from a night shift at work, Barbara heard things moving about in her room when she walked into it. She flicked on the light and saw Nora standing in the middle of her room. She was in her usual relaxed position, arms folded, just looking calmly towards Barbara. By the time Barbara got to me, the figure had disappeared."

When Mrs. Root's nephew was visiting them a short time ago, he was amazed one day to look up from a chair in the living room and see Nora coming down the stairs, turning into the hallway and then gliding back towards the kitchen.

Neighbors, too, noticed something strange one night. When the Roots were all out and the house was in darkness, a friend across the street observed that a decorative colonial candle Mrs. Root kept on the front window ledge was suddenly burning brightly. As she watched, the candle was then lifted up and carried from room to room in the house, until it was brought back and replaced on the sill, where the flame was extinguished and all became blackness again.

"I can now tell in other ways when Nora is here," adds Mrs. Root with a gracious smile. "I have awakened in the night or early morning hours to a strong scent of old fashioned cologne. Very sweet floral odor."

"Would you say a violet scent?" I asked.

"Yes, yes. I would say just that," she answered, pleased I had hit the identification so well.

"It was easy to do," I assured her, for I had caught the scent in the room very clearly myself when I first came in. It isn't a perfume one comes across much today.

"It certainly isn't one either Barbara or I use!" laughed my hostess.

Just a few days ago, I received a letter from Mrs. Root.

"Can there be more than one ghost in a house?" she asked. Twice, it seems, she and her daughter have seen a small girl about five or six years old. She is delicate, very small and has dark hair, though not as dark as Nora's.

I shall write her soon and explain that there can be any number of manifestations. Apparitions know no limits. Who is the child? Perhaps, Nora's daughter? Or even Nora, herself, as a little girl? Ghosts are hard to come by and when you do snare one or two, they can so easily defy detection.

But one thing is certain, in the late Victorian house on Ye Greate Street in Greenwich these fair phantoms will always be welcome.

A SMASHING SPIRIT

In a home at the other end of town a real ghost "character" seems to ramble around. One might even dub the haunting spirit a "no-good-prankster" and leave it at that.

I'm sure Willard and Ethel Hess would agree.

The Hess home is, like nearly every other one in the area, a historical landmark. Known as the "Jeremiah House," it was built in 1760.

But I would say it was more like 1970 before the old place took on its crazy, supernatural aspects.

The Hess family describes footsteps on the stairs; humming in the kitchen; laughter from the attic; things dropping heavily on the attic floor, like bricks; draperies left in a closed position found pulled open; a *click-click-click* sound on the banister as though someone were

snapping a stick along the length of it. And so forth, including the constant opening of doors left closed or locked and the annoying disturbance of pillows being thrown off the beds.

But eventually, the mischievous fellow did himself in, for Ethel Hess is a person who puts up with very little nonsense. The moment finally came when Ethel put her foot down and said, "Enough is enough!"

It was late at night not so long ago, when Mrs. Hess heard a loud crashing sound from the living room below. She was already half asleep, and in her state of semi-consciousness didn't feel too concerned, having heard so much mischief-making going on for so long. But, when the morning came and she walked into her living room and saw that her prize collection of antique bottles had been swept off her dough table and onto the floor, she felt the heat rise to her forehead.

"You little devil!" she shouted, "we're not going to go on living together in this house, I can tell you that! One of us has got to go and it's not going to be me! If you don't get yourself out of here, I'm going to call a medium or a priest or a witch or someone and they're going to exorcise you right into that old hot seat down there below and you know I mean what I say!"

Mr. Hess laughs when he recalls her heated ultimatum.

"It worked, too," he adds. "We've never had a thing happen since that night!"

I would say Mrs. Hess should leave her job in Bridgeton and go into the exorcism business.

At least the village will know where to turn if any of the Greenwich ghosts start acting too wild!

GHOST IN A HOUSEDRESS

Ghosts are usually attired in filmy nightdresses; dreamy-looking gowns or soft-hued velvets. I have heard of only one lady who was so casual as to make her re-appearance in this world in nothing more glamorous than a simple cotton housedress.

That's just what the spirit, if such it be, of a former resident of Feasterville, Pennsylvania, did in her earthbound home on Second Street Pike. So says one Jan Acker who ought to know. Jan lived in the old Victorian house and she once saw the previous owner appear years after the woman's demise.

"I had a real estate office in that building and I used to often work there late into the night. On such occasions, I'd hear footfalls upstairs along the hall and up and down the steps. So did my son, Larry.

Many a time, he'd hear knocking on his door upstairs and find no one was there.

"Well," continues Mrs. Acker, "I had always sensed someone's presence on the stair landing, but one night as I stepped into the hall, I looked up and caught sight of a matronly-looking woman just standing there, looking down at me. She was of medium height—maybe 5-foot five—with a pleasant face framed in silvery-gray hair. She was wearing a strand of pearls and a printed housedress. I can still see the pattern that was so clear to me then—little red roses on a navy blue background. She had one hand on the newel post and the other just hung at her side. She made no movement but just stared sweetly at me; then faded away.

"I understand from those who knew the former owner, who died in 1961, that was just the way she looked and the type of dress she liked to wear."

Mrs. Acker accepts the unusual nocturnal visitor with an understanding heart.

"The minute I stepped foot in this house, I felt a presence of some kind. I once had a medium come and she told me there are three ghosts here. One man and two women. I don't know who they all are, but I'm sure they're harmless. Like my lady in the housedress, they just like to come out once in a while and meet me! They don't bother me. I once saw my father come into my bedroom years ago. He'd been dead five months, yet I saw him distinctly. I figured it must mean something and it did. A short time later, my mother died. I think my dad came to warn me of that."

So ends the story of one Bucks County resident.

Whatever went on in the old Victorian house in Feasterville, the goodly spirits must find a new home soon. For the weather-beaten, paint-shy structure stands deserted now with "Danger" signs posted as a final appearance to the world before its demise at the hands of the wrecking ball.

Builders are not nearly as hospitable as sympathetic souls like Jan Acker.

A Demon in Delaware—Patty Cannon

The observance of Halloween in Dover, Delaware, has a rather sinister touch. The children can go to the Dover Public Library and satisfy their ghoulish little hearts all they want by gazing at a gaping skull that goes on display there every October thirty-first.

More heart-titillating than the sight of the skull are the tales that go with it. Tales that have been whispered in dusky tavern corners or retold over dying embers in a dark fireside hide-away for over a century and a half. Tales of one of the most brutal women who ever lived. Her name was Patty Cannon. And all that is left of her, fortunately, is her skull.

Patty Cannon was a slave-stealer. As owner of a tavern near the Maryland-Delaware border, she ran a bristling business in liquor, looseness and lives. Leading raids on surrounding fields, farms or towns, she snatched (hog-tying the victims herself) any and every Negro she caught sight of. The poor unfortunates were then chained in the "keep" attic of her tavern until a business deal selling them could be clinched.

Of the numerous accounts that were written about Patty, perhaps an article appearing in the November 9, 1930, edition of the *Baltimore Sun* sums it up best:

"Patty Cannon was… the Queen of Kidnappers. Her reign was the Dark Ages of the Eastern Shore, where her memory lingers, garish and bloody, from the mouth of the Susquehanna to the Cyprus swamps of the Pocomoke. After a hundred years she is still a nightmare to the back-country Negroes of Delaware and Eastern Maryland.

"'The First Lady of Crime' collected about her a prize lot of rascals as ever breathed. In her gang were graduates in atrocities from Baltimore and Philadelphia and the hardiest riffraff of the countryside. With these assorted rogues, she buccaneered up and down the peninsula, combing it for her prey."

In addition to the slave-selling, which netted handsome profits, sometimes a thousand dollars a head, Patty did a little murder on the side—if it promised rewards. And even if it didn't! One man carrying fifteen thousand dollars in cash ended up in her field six feet under, along with some children or sick adults that didn't make the grade in her trade.

All this horror finally came to a halt, when the aforementioned bodies were accidentally unearthed and Patty was hauled off to jail. *The Delaware Gazette* of April 17, 1829, carried the story. A great procession followed the black-haired, big-boned Amazon-of-a-woman to the Georgetown prison. There wasn't a townsperson within miles of the place that didn't hunger to know if Patty Cannon would weigh down the end of a noose. They were not to be satisfied. Before she could come up for trial, Patty took poison in her cell and died.

That old jail, in modern years, became the Sussex County Board of Assessment Building. The parking lot in the rear was originally the burial ground of the jail and was the resting place for Patty Cannon until the graveyard was done away with and the bodies moved to Potters Field. During that reburial process, the skull somehow became separated and fell into the hands of the local deputy sheriff. Today, it is on loan at the Dover Library where, as we have learned, it comes to daylight for blood-curdling recollections every Halloween.

Patty Cannon's tavern, her headquarters for the lethal operations, still stands, though heavily remodeled, in the little town of Reliance, Maryland, close to the Delaware border. It is privately owned and I have been assured no haunting spooks infest the premises today.

But still stories of ghosts persist. I heard that not long after Patty's death, a Baltimore lawyer, on a dare, spent the night in the deserted tavern. He didn't last the night. He was awakened by the sound of chains dragging across the floor of the attic above. On other occasions, travelers passing by the empty place reported seeing lights go on and off. Recently, I learned the Wilmington paper ran a story on the Patty Cannon ghost.

I have been told that Patty had a tunnel leading underground from her tavern in Maryland to an exit near the border in Delaware. By playing a kind of hop-scotch when the police came, for years she was able to elude their authority by being in the state where they could not arrest her. That tunnel, it is believed, still exists and spouts ghosts on moonlit nights into the surrounding countryside.

Who Walks at Woodburn?

If there are no Patty Cannon spooks below ground along the Maryland-Delaware border in the vicinity of Seaford, Delaware, one can't deny them authenticity in the cellar of the Governor's mansion at Dover, Delaware. They've been reported there for countless years, and with good reason. Woodburn was the scene of one of Patty Cannon's bloody slave raids. Any child in Dover can tell you this. It is their favorite sport on Halloween, to stare at the gruesome skull in the library, then run around the corner to Woodburn and keep an eye out for a Patty Cannon spook.

There's more of the spirit world roaming the Governor's mansion than the sights and sounds in the cellar. There's the famous apparition of a white-gowned bride who is occasionally glimpsed floating, not down an aisle, but, of all things, out a window!

Equally curious, is the report from time to time, that dinner guests at the mansion in past years have met strange people upstairs who were not seen again in the drawing room downstairs or later at the table in the candle-lit dining room. When they questioned who the roaming guests might be, the answer was always the same, "Oh, you have seen the permanent guests of Woodburn!"

Whether or not these guests from the past call on the Governor, I cannot say. Let's just be glad if Patty Cannon stays where she is.

The House that Wept

One of the most unforgettable conversations I have ever had was with a young boy, Andy Goldberg, a short time ago. He told me one of the eeriest, yet sweetest ghost tales I think I've ever heard.

I call it a love affair with a house.

Andy, with a friend, found what all young adventurers like to come upon... a deserted old farmhouse, back off a side road in their home town of Warminster, Pennsylvania. It had been a handsome structure with imposing grounds surrounding it. The outer buildings included a barn, corncrib, chicken coop, silo and what appears to have been a spring house or root-cellar storage area. Running along a section of the farm land from the

house to the barn, are the remains of a brick wall.

Andy and his friend chanced upon the old place very appropriately on a moon-drenched night. The two boys picked their way through weed-tangled cellar stairways and peered through gaping windows, reflecting back the white light in the sky to their awe-struck eyes.

"It was the weirdest feeling I've ever had," Andy told me in almost reverent tones. "That house, in spite of the state of disrepair and neglect, looked beautiful to me. All I could see was shining white paint and a straight-backed structure that was proud of itself, shimmering there in the moonlight."

The boys found a side door that opened with a groan. Inside, they stepped cautiously from room to room. They stared in silence at the bare walls and the dozens of wavy-glassed windows that blinked back at them in the glow from their flashlights like startled eyes long asleep and suddenly awakened.

Here and there in the corners, were empty coke bottles, cigarette butts and piles of trash left by previous interlopers.

Andy felt a surge of resentment at the thoughtlessness and lack of concern that had deposited such clutter in the lap of an ailing "lady." He vowed on the spot to return by daylight and clear up the debris.

And he did. Every afternoon he was free after school, he went over to the old farmhouse and spent the rest of the day gathering up the trash both inside the house and out; even around the outer buildings and along the dirt lane. Then he'd fill up his car with the vagrant debris and cart it off to the community dump.

With each trip, he came to love the place more.

"I feel that house is mine," Andy told me in wistful words. "I dream about fixing up her broken boards and polishing up the floor planks—they're so wide and beautiful. Oh, there are so many things I could do... but, of course, it never can belong to me," he added sadly. "Some builder bought it, I've heard. The house is going to be taken down."

Andy and his friend returned on a full moon night to say "goodbye" to his house. "Danger" and "No trespassing" signs would soon be up, he knew, nailed to the trunks of the high oaks and open-armed maples all along the lane.

The friend stayed in the car. Andy strolled listlessly down the dirt roadway, past the silent house. As he approached the broken framework of the corncrib opposite the low brick wall, he came to a standstill and looked around him. He felt immersed in thoughts too deep to explain, even to himself.

Then it began, a sound so faint that, at first, the boy thought it was the distant plaintive notes of some bird in a high tree top. Andy looked up and strained to listen better. Slowly the sound grew louder and more distinct. He couldn't believe his ears. It was no creature of the woods or fields; it was a human voice! A sad, whimpering. The crying of a young girl! The sound faded with an occasional choking as she stopped to catch her breath; then it would break out again, in a flood of hysterical weeping.

Spellbound, Andy turned and stared all about him. First, the crying came from the corncrib; then from the moonlit silo, high above him. Then it faded and dissolved into mere whimpering until it broke out afresh, this time from the torn windows of the house itself!

Andy pulled uncertainly backwards. "I know!" he found himself saying, "I know! But I can't help you! There is nothing I can do!"

The boy could feel the perspiration burst out on his forehead. He fought off a shudder for a moment, then he ran. He ran back to the car as fast as he could.

His friend had gotten out of his car and was looking up, listening. He appeared as surprised and mystified as Andy felt he was himself.

"Did you hear that? That weeping?" asked Andy.

"Sure did. What on earth was it? Is there some girl around here or something?"

Andy was staring up at the old house. "No," he answered thoughtfully, "there's no one. Only us."

"Then let's get the heck out of here," yelled the other boy as he shot back into the car and jerked it into gear.

Andy followed suit and they pulled out in a scuff of flying dirt, cut across the railroad tracks and back onto the main road.

The old Warminster house still stands there, awaiting the death knell, as so many old farms must do today. But, perhaps, not all of this beautiful lady will be lost and forgotten. For sure, Andy Goldberg will always remember her sad "goodbyes."

THE GHOST OF GRAEME PARK

Several years ago an item ran in a Philadelphia paper reporting a strange phenomenon. Pilots coming in for a landing at Willow Grove Naval Air Station just off Route 611 in Horsham had, on more than one occasion, observed a distracting and unexplainable green light flickering in fields below.

Pinpointing the disturbance, investigators found the weird lights came from the area of an old historic mansion off County Line— "Graeme Park."

The lights, it was determined, had nothing to do with the caretaker, the workmen, or the occasional visitors.

What were they? Investigators came up with a scientific answer, it is said. The green lights were a result of the phosphorus, commonly known as "will-o'-the-wisp," a familiar sight in the marshes of Scotland. In front of Graeme Park rests a serene pond. Behind it stretches a steam winding through the fields.

So what the pilots see as they come in for a landing is the will-o'-the-wisp hovering in the fields of Graeme Park.

Or is it?

There are some who will tell you otherwise. It is the ghost of beautiful Elizabeth Ferguson waiting for her love to return. She has been seen periodically through the centuries walking around the quiet waters of the pond, her green velvet skirts reflecting up from the moon-silvered water.

Her past lies in the history of the house itself. It began in 1717 when a Scottish baronet named Sir William Keith brought his family from England to Philadelphia. Sir William became a colonial Governor of Pennsylvania. He built himself a stately residence in Horsham Township and made it the finest and best known county seat in the area.

Sir William's guests were of the most famous of the day. His elegant four-horse carriage, his fine Madeira wine and his beautiful daughter, Ann, brought the admiration of everyone. Ann soon married Thomas Graeme, a canny Scots physician who had built up a lucrative practice in Philadelphia. Upon the death of Sir William—in a debtor's prison in England several years later—Ann Graeme took over as mistress of the house. The name of the mansion switched from the "Keith House" to "Graeme Park."

Ann and Thomas had an only child. She was the fragile and lovely Elizabeth. Her life, though she would seem to have everything— wealth, beauty and fame—became a tragic one.

She fell in love with a man in Philadelphia. No one knows his name, what he did, nor how she met him. Not even what happened to him.

The love affair faded in the mists of obscurity. All that is known is the sad fact that Elizabeth loved him deeply, but alas… her love was not returned. To forget him, she sailed to Scotland and lived there for some time. Before long, her mother, Ann Graeme, died and Elizabeth returned to America to take over the womanly duties of governing Graeme Park. They were busy sparkling days that followed. Benjamin Franklin sipped brandy at their hearthside.

Reverend White, who later became the Bishop of

Pennsylvania, visited them and a host of others whose names were to go down in history.

Elizabeth, now thirty-three years old, was an active hostess and had quite well forgotten her youthful heartbreak.

Then one day a young, handsome Scotsman walked in the door as a guest for a dinner party. He was twenty-three years old, had a dashing manner and words that enthralled as he spoke. He was an adventurer, he admitted as much. He also was quick to realize the advantages of having a bright and wealthy wife, even though she was many years his senior. It didn't take long for this charming, silver-tongued rogue to declare his undying love for the frail, sad-eyed woman who was the mistress of Graeme Park.

Dr. Graeme, aging as he was, understood the situation perfectly. He knew the antics of an opportunist when he saw them. He warned his daughter to beware.

But Elizabeth Graeme could no longer fight off the passion in her heart when she opened it wide to a lover's declarations. She adored Hugh Henry Ferguson with every fiber of her being. When he proposed, she wed him in secret, then carried the treasured deed quietly about with her as she lived on at Graeme Park.

One day Elizabeth made the difficult decision to tell her father of her marriage. She saw Dr. Graeme go out for his daily walk. She sat by a front window and watched him as he slowly strolled the mansion's surrounding pathways. It was autumn in the year 1772. She stared while the brown-tinged leaves whirled down upon the driveway. She took a breath for courage as she watched the doctor haltingly tread the path leading back to the house. He was getting nearer and nearer.

At that instant, suddenly he stopped, stretched his hands towards her, then pitched forward onto the walkway. When she reached him seconds later, he was dead.

Elizabeth Ferguson was plunged into grief. After the doctor's burial, the new master and his heavy-hearted bride settled down to oversee the estate of Graeme Park.

Tragedy for Elizabeth had just begun. The American Revolution broke out. Everywhere citizens were taking up arms or arguments for or against the cause of independence. Not made of the mettle to fight back against anything, but rather to accept things as they were, the frail Elizabeth could not be a part of the American struggle. She could see only preserving peace and the status quo.

Her husband, Hugh, felt a momentary twinge at declaring himself a Tory. After all, he had an American wife and was living luxuriously on American money. But the twinge was only brief. The rebels around him were only misguided fools. The insurrection itself would be quelled within months. With that, Hugh Henry Ferguson joined the British service. His wife never laid eyes on him again.

Many years later, she learned the adventurous devil had died in battle in the Flemish wars.

Elizabeth Ferguson moved further into tragedy. By a strange twist of fate, the good intentions she bore for everyone and everything seemed only to backfire in a cloud of confusion and error. In an attempt to help America from a rebellion of extinction as she saw it, she offered to serve as a messenger on a peace proposal to General George Washington from the faint-hearted Reverend Duche of Philadelphia. The clergyman penned the suggestion that the cause for independence was hopeless and recommended that the General compromise with the British. Furious when he read the contents, Washington denounced the letter, its author and its bearer in a communication to Congress.

Duche departed to the safer climate of England. Mrs. Ferguson stayed on at Graeme Park, looked upon with suspicion by all about her.

Her threads of involvement were not yet strained badly enough to be broken. Against her better judgment, she was implicated in a new plan by Governor George Johnstone, a commissioner appointed by Parliament to settle, if possible, the differences between America and Great Britain. Johnstone asked Mrs. Ferguson to visit General Reed of the American forces. She was to tell him that if he would exert his influence to quell the rebels' ire, he would command ten thousand guineas and the best post under the English government.

Elizabeth hesitated. Much as she wished to do all she could to establish peace, would not General Reed look upon such a mode of obtaining his influence as a bribe?

"No bribe, my dear Madame," replied Johnstone. "Such a mode of proceeding is common in all such negotiations, and one may honorably make it a man's interest to step forth in Britain's cause."

With misgivings, but with the desire to help, Elizabeth requested and obtained an interview. The result of it has gone down in the history books. After hearing the proposition, General Reed stretched to his full height and scorched out a reply to Mrs. Ferguson. "I am not worth purchasing; but such as I am, the King of Great Britain is not rich enough to do it!"

The act of Elizabeth's spread throughout the colonies. It was labeled "treason." She was scorned in the newspapers; taken to task by Congress. Word grew that Mrs. Ferguson had undertaken the proposition in order to secure a better position for her husband in the British service. Governor Johnstone hightailed it back to England, where he sent word that Mrs. Ferguson's story of the incident was a bundle of misunderstanding and misquotes as to his part.

Elizabeth Ferguson lived on at Graeme Park in quiet and loneliness. Although constantly suspect in the eyes of her neighbors, she did what little she could for her fellow Americans. She spun a quantity of linen day after day in her empty parlor where once the great people of that age had chatted and sipped wine. Now she worked steadily, spinning linen which she made into shirts for the sparsely-clad American prisoners brought into Philadelphia after the Battle of Germantown.

The years that pulled Elizabeth into old age were no kinder than the earlier ones. She lost most of her fortune, then finally the home she loved—Graeme Park. She spent her last days in the home of a charitable friend not far from her beloved mansion. She died, and welcomed death, it was said, in February of 1801.

Is it any wonder that moonlit nights silvering the dark fields and the cold walls of Graeme Park and the oval pond find a solitary figure wandering along the mossy edges of the water? Does not Elizabeth Ferguson deserve the quiet stroll after her lifetime of disappointment?

Does she seek her young girlhood lover? Her adventurous husband? Her beloved father? Or does she still seek what she could not find in life… peace and understanding?

GHOSTLY CAPERS AROUND CAPE MAY

Cape May, New Jersey, has been an active Delaware Bay town ever since its founding by New England whalers many long years ago. A fact that easily explains its early name, "New England Town." Today, centuries later, the whole area of Cape May County seems to be abounding in ghostly lore and legend... enough to satisfy any ghost-chaser as romantic as myself.

FULL MOON GHOST

I started my jaunt at Cape May Court House and learned from an old townsperson, whose path I so fortuitously crossed, that he once had first-hand dealings with a Cape May ghost in his own house! It seems a clipper ship captain of the late 1800s, who had built his home in Cape May Court House, was lost at sea and never returned to his beloved abode. The house was closed up and locked. Weeds and bushes took over the grounds and, ultimately, so did the old captain's restless spirit.

"I've felt it myself," my charming informant told me. "It's a feeling you can't describe—to feel a presence the way I have."

"What exactly happens?" I asked.

"Well, every full moon, like clock work, the house comes alive with weird noises. The windows rattle; the stairs creak—the very walls groan. It's as though the house wants to cry out its anguish. Of course, on such nights I can't sleep. I just lie awake wondering what those walls are trying to say. Maybe the old captain went down under a full moon, so he comes back home just as he wished he could those long years ago during his last thoughts? Who knows?"

Who, indeed, does?

THE HAUNT OF HIGBEE HOUSE

I made my way from Cape May Court House, down the Cape, towards Cape May town itself. The quiet streets, the empty sand stretches, the old world houses were a rare treat, so peaceful out of season. A short distance from the resort town lies "Higbee's Beach," scarcely noted today. In the 1600s, it was a whaling station called "Higbee's Landing." An inn was established there in subsequent years known as the "Higbee House." It is reputed that the oldest part of the inn once belonged to William Penn. He is believed by historians of this area, to have landed at this spot and bought a home there prior to his moving up the Delaware to Bucks County, where he later settled.

Higbee House consisted of three sections—the old "William Penn part" and two subsequent additions. One man to whom I spoke recalled well the tales about the old inn. His father had related to him many times, the story that Delaware Bay pirates (including, of course, Captain Kidd) landed at Higbee's Beach. They hauled their captives to the old Penn House, chaining them to the garret walls to await ransom.

In true buccaneer style, they usually sailed off, leaving the unfortunate prisoners chained and forgotten to rot on the spot.

It seems the unhappy spirits of these captives would never leave well enough alone in the years when the structure came to serve as an inn. Late at night travelers staying at the tavern were awakened by the eerie sounds of chains rattling and dragging across the attic flooring.

Today, the spot seems to have settled into eternal quiet. Nothing is left of the ancient "resort" but a decaying ice house and a few scattered stones.

Town Bank's Eerie Stairway

Moving up the Cape along the Delaware, I drove to Town Bank, where once stood a structure known as the Town Bank House—a building no one in the village today seems to have heard of. It was, nevertheless, according to an old Cape May historian whom I befriended, once a site visited by William Penn in 1680. My friend said his father used to talk about strange doings in that house. Late on moonless nights, people in that house (and he himself once witnessed it, I gathered) heard a sickening thumping sound of something rolling down the old stairs. Once the bottom was reached, the front door would fly open. And that was it! Always the same routine. A Thump! Thump! Thump!, down each step, until the bottom; then the front door would swing wide open, and would remain open until some living creature had nerve enough to shut it.

Golder's Hole and its Fiery Spook

A few miles beyond Cold Spring, I found myself in another ghost-riddled area; a spot known years ago as "Golder's Hole." The section is located in the village called "Sally Marshall's Crossing." A villager told me that years ago the whole swampy, mist-laden area was considered a spook-infested haunt.

At the edge of the swamp once stood, long ago, an old house with a tumble-down porch clothed in wild vines and long-tenacled weeds. This man remembered hearing of one particular weird incident. A friend of his, while passing the Golder's Hole deserted house, saw a great ball of radiating light roll out of the swamp, swing up onto the porch, cross to the other side and leap into the misty, watery ground beyond and vanish.

"Townspeople claimed it was some pirate's fiery spirit trying to escape the swamps where he'd been thrown."

One thing is sure, there were pirates all around Delaware Bay.

Local newspapers of centuries ago abound with reports of their presence in the Bay and in the Delaware River itself. In the Cape May County Historical Museum one can see today the silver-muzzled pistol considered to be one of Captain Kidd's.

For all I learned of the region, I'm willing to believe Captain Kidd himself still stalks the sands and stretches of the Cape looking for his buried treasure—or even his favorite silver pistol!

The Eyes of Old Brick Church

Backtracking along Town Bank's main road, I found myself in the village of Cold Spring. There's a haunt there, too, in a church no less. At least, there was over half a century ago. The church is the Cold Spring Presbyterian Church, affectionately known as the "Old Brick Church." A man I spoke to told me his father had heard from the sexton, Furman Garretson, that there were haunting spirits down in the basement. The sexton had seen them on several occasions. They were shaped like monsters with huge eyes that burned right through you. Though he never hung around long enough on such occasions to see how badly they could burn!

The Lost Silver Mine

A short distance north of Willow Grove on Old York Road, in Montgomery County, Pennsylvania, is a hill known in wilderness days as "Huckleberry Hill" from the abundance of whortleberry bushes growing there.

It soon grew a far more intriguing product—the legend of a silver mine.

In 1683, William Penn purchased this area from Chief Wessapoak and a sparse collection of colonists trickled in. From those earliest times, the region came to be regarded as haunted or under a spell. It seems Chief Wessapoak waxed most unhappy about parting with his land to Penn, for it contained valuable minerals. Before dying, the chief uttered a curse that no good should ever come to any white man who desired to procure riches thereon.

The chief read the heart of the white man well. The settlers soon became obsessed with the idea of wresting wealth from Huckleberry Hill. It was an idea that sprang from an old tale. The tale of a hidden silver mine.

The story of the silver mine dates back to 1697, when a Captain Hans Moen is said to have sailed up Pennepack Creek into this region in search of a silver mine he learned of from the Indians. What success he achieved has become lost in the fogbank of antiquity. Other treasure seekers followed in his wake throughout the centuries. None ever met with results.

The legend of the mine centers on the story of a farmer named Derrick Kroons. He was of German descent, his father being one of the early settlers from the Palatinate region. Kroons lived about a half-mile from a ravine near the crest of Huckleberry Hill. He lived in a stone house surrounded by a well, a garden, a beehive and a log barn, all tied neatly together by a white-washed clapboard fence.

Kroons was a good husband, a hard worker and a man of ambition. And nothing fed this ambition more readily than the hours he spent thinking about the silver mine story of Huckleberry Hill.

One December night, as the handful of neighbors joined together around a warm fire at the old homestead of Derrick Kroons, the talk turned to the mine.

"Sure it is," murmured an Irishman, "that silver exists in these parts. Silver has already been found in the Sierra Madre mountains of New Spain, so 'tis logical the same vein extends into the Alleghenies and thence to Blue Ridge and on through Edgehill and finally, at last, to Huckleberry Hill!'"

The men puffed on their pipes and leaned forward on their elbows.

"Aye," said another, "And there's Anthony Larry, the water diviner... me thinks he has found with his divining rod more than the proper spot to dig a well! Aye, he's found the silver mine itself, there's no doubt. Have ye noticed the tone of his great silver shoe buckles? They be of virgin ore if ever I spied it."

"Ah, yes," agreed a neighbor, "if we could find the silver mine there would be no further necessity for us to toil. We could all hold our heads high. We'd own country seats and fine coaches like the Hamiltons, Allens, Morrises and Logans."

In a few hours the men parted company.

But Derrick Kroons, who had said nothing all through the fireside discussion, made a pact with himself. As he lay his head down that night he promised himself he would lend every effort towards finding the silver mine.

All through the following winter, Derrick searched and searched. By March he had fixed upon what he considered must be the spot—the ravine, no farther than about a half-mile from his house. For several days then he would depart early in the morning with a miner's pick in hand and head for the woods bordering the ravine.

He would not return until night. No one—not even his wife—knew where he went, nor dared to ask.

One night he didn't return.

His wife was puzzled. Murders were practically unknown; Indians in that region were friendly. She turned to the Kroons' farmhand, Fritz. He gathered neighbors together and within a few hours of dawn a search party was on its way.

Fritz took the hillside in the thick woods near to the farm. For hours his feet stepped carefully through the tangled underbrush. No man relished being alone on Huckleberry Hill when the darkness began to fall, and dusk was now fast coming on. The March wind shook the winter-dried branches about him like the death rattle of a snake. Fritz edged cautiously down the sides of the ravine. Suddenly something brushed his face.

It was Derrick Kroons' coat, swaying like a scarecrow from a bare branch.

Fritz dropped his eyes and scanned the underbrush. Soon he was in a small clearing. A hole in the earth, big enough to trap a deer, gaped unexpectedly before his eyes. To one side lay a heap of dirt. From out of it, he caught sight of a white hand stretched out and grasping on to a tree root. Then Fritz saw the stone-still, waxen features of Derrick Kroons projecting out from the pile of freshly-dug dirt.

Fritz shoveled in frantically. By the time dark had settled down, the farmhand was on his way back to the farm with Derrick slung over his shoulders.

Derrick Kroons lived. He was cold, stiff, bruised and speechless when they laid him on his bed. But he lived. His wife nursed him back to health. The neighbors, finding nothing of value in the hole Derrick had dug, filled it in again.

Derrick Kroons, it is said, never spoke again.

What evil befell him as he was digging? A wild animal? An unfriendly neighbor?

These questions were the talk of Huckleberry Hill for generations. The story of the "Silver Mine of Huckleberry Hill" persisted until late in the 1800s. When farms in that area went up for sale, with the selling went the saying, "There's sure to be silver on it!"

Today, only Silver Lake of York Road serves to remind us of the glittering legend. Or the shrill shriek of some youngster from the banks of the Neshaminy where he has happened upon some mica particles.

"Wow! Silver!"

Whole Lot of Tossin' and Turnin' Goin' On

When one gets deep in psychic investigation it is fascinating to observe similarities and patterns that occur in haunting manifestations, across not only geographical differences, but across time spans as well.

One of these repetitions involves the wild movements of nothing less than a lady's hairbrush! The flight of the object in question seems in both cases (over a century apart) to set off a series of strange occurrences.

The first happened in the year 1866 in a house on South Fifth Street in Philadelphia. The father, the owner of a small dry-goods store in the city, had moved with his wife and three young daughters to the South Fifth Street house some ten years earlier. It had been a happy and peaceful decade. Then on the early morning of February first, the haunting phenomena began.

All three daughters, who shared a bedchamber, awoke suddenly to a strange clattering sound close beside them. They all sat up, looked at each other, then around the room. On the floor, they spotted their gleaming silver-backed hair brushes!

"How in the world—?" exclaimed the oldest who, scratching her long hair with a thoughtful gesture, decided to jump out of bed and replace each of their brushes on its respective chest of drawers.

She had no sooner hopped back into her bed, when a louder clattering than before brought all three girls to a sitting position once more. Their hairbrushes and all their combs and hand-mirrors, as well as vanity bottles, silver-backed nail buffers and nail files, lay strewn around the floor, as though thrown by some child in a tantrum.

They each got out of bed and searched around the room—peering into closets, through windows, and into the hallway. They could find nothing. It was so early, and since their parents were still sound asleep, the girls decided to say nothing till later. They left everything just where it had fallen and climbed back into bed discussing the strange incident until the sun was up, clear and bright. They were about to get out of bed for the last time when, without any warning, they saw a large gilt-framed looking glass which hung on the wall, jump off the large supporting hook and fly to the corner of the room, where it fell to the floor in a thousand pieces.

In one sweeping wave, the girls rushed out of their room and into their parents' bedroom, where they shrieked out their terror.

Neither the father nor the mother could think of any solution to the bizarre incident, other than to speculate that one of the girls must have been sleep-walking and the other two in a dream state.

It wasn't long until the whole family saw for themselves there was no dream involved. The next evening as the family sat around the parlor, all the bric-a-brac on the fireplace mantel danced wildly about, banging into each other like huge, colorful Mexican jumping beans! As tiny bits of glass flew around the place, the mother hastily removed some of the objects to the floor. To no avail.

The large mirror hanging on the chimney wall leaped off its nail, took a zig-zag flight across the room and smashed to bits against the opposite wall.

Hardly had they recovered their wits from this stunning attack, when the mother and one daughter, trying to set the table for dinner, found themselves completely unable to do so. The plates jumped off the table; a pitcher of water flew up and struck the girl on the forehead; and a loaf of bread, as lively as a spinning top, whirled across the table top in a crazy path.

That was too much. The family grabbed their wraps and hysterically rushed to a neighbor's house.

The strange doings in the South Fifth Street house, from that time on, made headlines in the local papers and were the subject of talk everywhere in Philadelphia, from the butcher shop to the church pulpit. But no matter how much talk went on, no solutions to the mystery were forthcoming.

As members in good standing of a nearby Baptist Church, the

family requested, and got, the attention of their pastor. He came to investigate along with a fellow clergyman. They fared no better than the members of the family. The moment after they entered the parlor, a hymn book was projected from a table where there was no one standing nearby and pitched itself violently against a door. When the pastor retrieved the book and placed it back on the table, it flew off again, this time accompanied by a Bible. Later the same performance occurred involving a prayer book as well. All three books whirled around the room, out the door, around the rest of the house, and upon returning, made a full stop against the parlor wall.

Neither visitor was able to discover any trick by which such action could have taken place. Later, police and reporters so filled the house and curious crowds so packed the outside, that the family finally had to move to preserve their sanity.

Similar to this "poltergeist" or "mischievous spirits" activity, is the disturbance that occurred during the spring and winter of 1972 in the beautiful historic home of Ann and Charles Miller in Newtown, Pennsylvania.

Rich with centuries-old traditions, this gracious structure houses not only priceless antiques procured by Mr. Miller (a prominent interior decorator in the Philadelphia area), but also a ghost or two, as well.

The first I heard of any unusual happening was the day Mrs. Miller called to tell me about a strange incident. The night before, as she was preparing to retire for bed, she was hanging up a dress in her closet and, suddenly, she noticed her silver-backed hairbrush flying off the vanity top and hurling itself across the room! The brush plopped right into her husband's lap who, at the time, was sitting up in bed reading.

"Neither one of us was anywhere near the dressing table at the time! It seemed utterly unbelievable! Yet, it did happen!"

I assured Ann Miller that I knew it did. It brought to my mind a recollection of the previous incident, but I said nothing, hoping that the silver brush activity would be the end of it. It wasn't.

A few days later, I learned from Charles that a light shining into his eyes awoke him from a sound sleep in the middle of the night. He forced his tired eyes open and was amazed to see one of Ann's vanity lamps shining brightly under its organdy shade! He couldn't believe his eyes, for he knew his wife had snapped off both lamps before she'd retired that night. He got up and clicked the light off, returning to bed. A short time later, he awoke again. The same light was gleaming away at him through the darkness.

The next morning, Charles examined the light and its switch. There was nothing wrong.

I hoped that would be the end of it—but it wasn't.

Less than a month later when the Millers let themselves in after a brief trip away, they soon became conscious of a strange whirring sound floating down from the floor above.

"By gosh, I think some bird's gotten in and is trapped in the den upstairs," commented Charles.

Ann shrugged and looked at him. "Well, let's go see."

Slowly, they edged up the stairs, rounded the tiny bend to the den's entrance and peered in. The room was empty. But the sound was more distinct.

Charles glanced up at the loft area, just above the den.

"I think it's coming from up there." He eased up the tiny stairway and shot a look about the storage area. There were suitcases,  packing boxes, unused pieces of furniture, holiday decorations and some tools. And, oh yes, an old Victrola from Charles' college days. Covered with dust and webbed with those lacy filaments that all attic objects collect, it sat now right where he'd placed it years ago—on top of an old table.

He reached out to it, incredulous. The turntable was revolving! Unused and long since completely wound down, it seemed utterly impossible that it could be in operation. But it was. The whole mechanism was humming as sprightly as it had over thirty years ago!

"There's been a lot that's happened in this old house over the centuries," commented Ann. "Do you suppose there could be something still here, remaining in the atmosphere, so to speak, to reactivate itself to us?"

Was an answer to this question supplied a short time later, when a group of us held a séance in the quiet candle-lit house one cold snow-crusted night?

KYW-TV was present and recorded the event for its show, *On the Rare Side*. Jack Helsel, Carol Fisher and their staff, as well as the renowned medium, Grace Walker, myself, and a choice circle of psychics all gathered about a blazing hearth. We waited.

The air seemed full of voices wanting to speak. To Mrs. Walker and to several others, they did. Mrs. Walker "saw" an old sea chest in the center of the room. "And I get the sensation of waves," contributed a male psychic. Mr. Miller nodded. The first builder of the house in the 1800s had come from France. He would have brought just such a chest. Then Grace Walker said she felt that someone who was connected with the house in the past was also related in some way to a restraining force—imprisonment, perhaps. Again, Charles Miller agreed. Napoleon's aide, Joseph Archambault, who had been in island exile with the General, was the original builder of the house. It is believed on many occasions he and Joseph Bonaparte, Napoleon's brother, visiting from Bordentown across the Delaware, along with fellow compatriots, had conspired in that room to free their General and bring him to America.

Later, Mrs. Walker looked up towards the far wall of the room. "I just saw a woman come through that wall. She's dressed in a long black gown with full skirts. She looks terribly sad."

Ann Miller signaled Grace Walker. "That sounds like Violetta. She was living here in the last century. She was a sister to the famous primitive painter, Edward Hicks."

"And," added Charles, "there used to be an entrance door on that side of the room. It was walled over years ago."

Another psychic woman in the group spoke up. "I think she drowned here, that lady. I feel the water as though it were in my own lungs."

"You're right," contributed the historical expert, Charles Miller. "Violetta heard the cries of her drowning son in the creek outside.

She ran down and plunged in, desperately trying to save the child. The boy was rescued by a passerby but Violetta, weighed down by her full heavy skirts, sank too quickly to be saved. They pulled her out and carried her to the bedchamber upstairs. She died there."

Ann looked up and added quickly, "that is our room, the room where my silver hairbrush flew off the vanity and the light went on!"

Later, in the upstairs den, Mrs. Walker could not stay in the room. "I can't stay here a minute longer," she complained. "A terrible, thundering noise keeps reverberating in my ears. It's deafening and head-splitting. Something dreadful happened in this room at one time."

Charles admitted that Grace was all too right. "The whole roof over that room once collapsed, crushing everything under it. Fortunately, no one was in it at the time."

Grace nodded. "I heard it," she murmured, "I heard it falling."

Fortunately, the house is tranquil these days for the Millers. Whoever, or whatever, wrought its mischief in that atmosphere never came again after our midnight investigation. Have the restless spirits in that house been quieted forever? I must say, in my heart, I feel all is well.

GHOSTS THAT DARKEN DELAWARE STATE

While researching the ways and byways of Delaware state, I came across the two following ghost tales of the area.

An old home stands in the countryside that goes back to the late 1600s. In fact, this estate was part of a William Penn grant. A descendant, who occupied the house in later years, was a landowner of means and a man of stature in the community. He apparently was also a scoundrel. Legend says that for some unknown reason, his anger was once so aroused against his own granddaughter that he killed her in a fit of rage.

Then he dragged her down the back stairs that night, pulling her through a secret tunnel leading away from the house, until he reached the outside grounds. Under the cover of darkness, he lifted her body up over the stone wall of a well and threw her into the inky depths.

He waited a moment, listening stiffly to the resounding splash echoing in the deep shaft, then quietly returned to the house the same way he had come out.

No one ever seemed to be the wiser.

But all the same, it seems, he continues to pay for his crime. Periodically, through the subsequent centuries, occupants of the historic home, and even visitors to the place, declare they have heard weight-laden footsteps plunging wearily along the tunnel.

One woman I spoke to said she had a friend who has seen the dastardly fellow in question. She was staying at the old home not so many years ago when, quite unexpectedly, she looked up to see a man in breeches and jacket and lace-trimmed wrists, staring at her as though she were a most uninvited intruder. Then his form faded until it melted away completely. This happened, I was told, on three different occasions while she was visiting in the venerable haunt.

I was told by several different residents of the town about another haunted house off the main square in the heart of New Castle. Different owners there over the years have been troubled by the sound of somebody walking around on the third floor. Even a neighbor next door, reputedly, has heard the footsteps at times when she knew the old frame house was empty. The present tenants have checked and rechecked for trapped squirrels or birds or broken tree limbs. Nothing concrete has been found that could be the cause. I talked to the owner who admitted with a half-smile, he had, when living there, heard strange sounds late at night.

Who it is who so restlessly and relentlessly paces the tiny upstairs quarters, nobody seems to know. At least, it is another intriguing tale to add to Delaware's dark side.

THE GHOST WOLF

The legends in Bucks County, Pennsylvania, are legion. Something about the very name conjures up an atmosphere of the fireside tale; the haunted hill; the shadowy Never-Never Land of the half-truth or the whole myth, and the fascinating folktale realm.

One of the least known and slimmest of tales is the story of the "Wolf Ghost of Burn Bridle Hill" in Solebury Township. The very name of the hill and forest there is legend. Some reported that it was so called because the Indian name for it sounded similar.

Others said it came from the fact that when Washington set up headquarters in Bucks, prior to crossing the Delaware on Christmas night in '76, the British, encamped at the foot of the hill, burned the bridles and saddles of their horses to keep the Americans from getting them. Another story says it arose from a tragic fire that occurred there in early days and the settlers dubbed it "Burn Bridle Hill."

Be that as it may, Burn Bridle Hill had more than an intriguing name—it had a ghost. A wolf ghost!

The story came to light, thanks to the written recollections of an elderly Bucks County lady named Mrs. Annie Pearson Darrow of Altadena, California, who was born and raised in Solebury Township. George MacReynolds published her account in his book, *Place Names in Bucks County*.

After discussing the history of the name of the hill, which we have just covered, Mrs. Darrow added, "There was a ghost story in connection with the hill, too."

She goes on to tell us the tale that began back in the days when the Lenni-Lenape Indians hunted the forests of Bucks. It seems that in that hillside area a vicious wolf roamed, devouring any flesh that crossed his path. He finally killed several Indian children. The Indians would not rest until they had tracked down the beast and finished him off. The band of hunters surrounded the animal at a point where, in Mrs. Darrow's lifetime, the road from Forrest Crooks meadow "joined the main road through the forest." There the hunters accomplished the fatal deed.

Ever after, however, the ghost of the wolf was said to haunt that spot. Wilson Pearson, Mrs. Darrow's father, recalled to his daughter how fearful the residents of the locality were at night during his boyhood years. He could remember how terrified they were at the thought of going outside after dark.

Mrs. Darrow stated that, fortunately, neither she nor any members of her family who lived in Solebury ever found themselves face to face with the animal's pale and frightful specter.

But who can dismiss the "Wolf Ghost of Burn Bridle Hill" just like that?

Surely, the wary listener on moonlit nights traveling up York Road from Buckingham to Solebury can hear the blood-freezing howling of the murderous wolf still clinging to the dark night.

One more legend of Bucks to be polished bright again and cherished in the searching mind.

APPARITIONS IN THE APARTMENT

In November of 1971, I received a letter from a charming woman of Philadelphia who lives in a haunted apartment. Her name is Mrs. J. Allyson and she proceeded to recount to me a fascinating experience. In fact, as time rolled on and I heard from her a number of times, the phenomena became more intriguing.

It seems that one Friday afternoon that November, Mrs. Allyson sat down in her apartment living room to watch the David Frost television show. She looked at her watch; took note it was some minutes until four, and decided to read the afternoon newspaper awhile.

She scanned the news only a minute or two when something made her look up from the paper. She was astonished to see a woman standing across the room from her. She was short of stature, scarcely five feet tall and fully dressed in a raincoat and hat. The hat was flat and pressed down over her dark hair.

Much to her own amazement, Mrs. Allyson didn't feel any shock or even surprise. It seemed only right, somehow, for that woman to be standing there. She didn't project the feeling that she was an intruder. Mrs. Allyson found herself wrapped in wonderment, but not fear. Though she was curious who the woman was, she couldn't open her mouth to utter a word.

So the two women stared at each other silently, as long seconds ticked on. The clear eyes, focused so relentlessly on Mrs. Allyson, seemed questioning. Yet, what was on her mind? The guest said nothing and Mrs. Allyson simply was not able to speak.

In another second, the woman in the raincoat started walking slowly across the room. As she got closer to where Mrs. Allyson was sitting, she took a small step downwards as though descending from some invisible raised platform or stair landing. A half-smile appeared on her face for a fraction of a second; then she turned away towards the wall and disappeared into a silver-streaked nothingness.

Out of habit, Mrs. Allyson picked up her paper again, then dropped it back into her lap as she murmured out loud to herself... *"I have just seen a ghost!"*

Nor was that afternoon in November to be the last time.

Not many weeks after the unusual incident, Mrs. Allyson looked up at her television screen one evening and had a fleeting impression of a woman's form passing between it and her. She was in a filmy gown and carried something in her left hand. Then she was gone!

But a visual apparition of a woman is not the only manifestation in the Philadelphia apartment. Mrs. Allyson many times hears a humming sound at night in her bedroom. It is the lisping meanderings of a woman's voice, as though she were humming while doing some small task, or perhaps rocking a baby in her arms.

Mrs. Allyson decided to do some detective work. She located a woman who knew a great deal about the apartment. Her sister had lived there, and—most interesting to the new tenant—had died there in the bedroom some years ago.

Further investigation revealed that the apartment building stands today on the same site as the mansion of an old aristocratic Philadelphia family.

Was the woman in the apparition the neighbor's sister; or was she a long-forgotten resident of that earlier domicile? Had she worked in the mansion at one time? Was she coming back to find someone or something?

Mrs. Allyson spent the subsequent months thinking back frequently on the experiences of last year. Then a remarkable incident occurred again the following spring, plunging her deeper into questioning than ever before.

She was sitting in the same armchair in the living room, as on the previous occasion, and at the same hour. It was a Thursday afternoon in May of 1972. Suddenly she felt compelled to look up, just as she had before. This time she saw the vague outline of a face.

Then it gradually filled in with the features of a young man. He had dark hair and was wearing glasses. He was most attractive and he looked straight at her.

He said nothing either, but simply stared at Mrs. Allyson as he fumbled with his eyeglasses, as though unusually conscious of them. He appeared to be sitting down and Mrs. Allyson was aware that she saw only his face and shoulders. For a long moment, he just sat there gazing at her, then slowly he dissolved into thin air and was gone.

As before, Mrs. Allyson was overcome with wonder but felt no fear.

"I have no concern over their visits," she says, "only, perhaps a little bewilderment. Why have these people come to me?"

Mrs. Allyson still has not found the answer to that question. She continues to seek it, though. As of last report to me, the visitors have not come again to call.

The future, however, may be something else again!

HAUNTED FRATERNITY HOUSE

On a side street in Trenton, New Jersey, stands an old row home that today harbors a fraternity of Mercer County Community College.

No fraternity house ever boasted a more exciting roster of events than this one according to several of the boys who live there, and they ought to know. Supernatural events, they mean... of course.

It all began in June of 1968 when one of the boys, Criss, in his third floor room, awoke in the middle of the night to find his bed shaking violently. He jumped out and examined it carefully. It stopped quivering. He looked out the small rear window over the roof tops to see if he could detect any sign of a storm, thunder or lightning, or even a heavy truck passing by. Anything that might have caused the extraordinary vibrations. He could detect none of those things and he returned to bed, puzzled.

Shortly after this occurrence, he was studying late one night when he clearly heard footsteps pacing the floors overhead. A remarkable sound for sure, as the attic floors had long since been removed! The young man didn't know what to make of it, but nothing else happened for a long time and soon he forgot the strange events.

Two years went by and life went on as usual in the fraternity house—hard work, happily spiced with parties.

But no ghostly doings, until one unforgettable night in the spring of 1970. That night Criss awoke to see a black dove flying from corner to corner in his room!

The boy sat bolt upright.

"I was never superstitious or a believer in spiritualism or anything like that, but, man, I tell you I could only think someone was sending me a message from the Other Side that night!"

Criss hadn't mentioned anything to anyone for some time. But then the incident of the black dove kept reoccurring for several subsequent nights. Of course, when he investigated, there was no such creature in the room.

Finally, he told a girlfriend about it. Her parents were European, and people of the Old World don't dismiss such occurrences.

"Put salt behind your door, Criss, and hang a cross on the front of the door," she ordered. "Mama says to."

Criss laughed and said he'd think about it.

From that time on, things seemed to "pop" all over the house. Weird things happened—one after another. A pair of white tennis shoes Criss had soaking in a pail of bleach disappeared, reappearing later in a locked and unoccupied room beneath his. Another time, one of his buddies walked into the bedroom and suddenly noticed that the brass headboard of Criss' bed was vibrating like mad. The boy left abruptly and never went back.

One day when Criss returned from the shower, he found all his clothes that he had laid out on the bed, missing. Later, he found them in a drawer.

Criss tells of the time another one of the boys in the house, who was alone on the second floor, heard the front door below open and close and footsteps come up the stairs. When he checked to see who was there, he found no one. He was still alone!

Another time, a buddy walked into a room where Criss was standing and for a moment saw the form of someone else standing behind Criss. Then the figure disappeared.

Finally, as a constant aggravation to one as neat as Criss, the young man kept finding his belongings moved. A cigarette lighter would not be where he left it. The rulers on his desk would be scattered. His lamps moved from their accustomed places. His radio alarm set at 4 A.M. instead of the usual time. All this accented with sundry knocking and rattling sounds from windows and walls.

Criss was becoming annoyed to the point of complete exasperation, when an experience occurred which he will never forget.

He was lying in bed, not quite asleep, when he opened his eyes and looked towards a far corner of his room. He pointed upwards to me, as he recounted the tale, showing me the exact spot.

"There," he said, "right there, I saw the shadowy form of a man hanging! It was just the figure from the waist up, but it was distinct. His neck was twisted sideways, the way it is thrown when a noose breaks the neck from a sudden drop!"

Criss shook his head at me. "Man, that's when I got some salt and threw it behind the door and hung a cross up right where you can see it now!"

"Did it help?"

"Well, not really. The next night, I think it was, I awoke from the heavy weight of something pressing on my chest and stomach. It was so powerful, I gasped for air. It was someone or something all right. I could feel its hot breath against my face... "

The next step was a suggestion from a friend, to hold a séance in the room. Criss did just that. In fact, several séances. The final one was with three mediums from the area. What did they all unearth?

Several events from the past, if the spiritualists are to be believed. One centered around a young girl named "Martha" who described the house as she had known it centuries ago and the Trenton streets with sights and sounds as they had been to her.

The other ghostly presence was named "Frederick." He, it seems, was responsible for beating his sister to death in the early years of this century. But, before he did her in, she evened the score by slipping him a little cyanide so that he died, too.

I am told newspaper accounts of the foregoing incident appeared in the Trenton papers years ago.

Are "Martha" and "Frederick" the ghosts who visit the old fraternity house? Criss still doesn't know.

Aside from seeing a mirror go black, then white; and a form hanging in the corner once again; and baseboards shining in the dark as well as books on the shelf glowing as if covered with phosphorescence; and a man's scream from a locked room in the dead of night—most of life in the fraternity house in Trenton seems to have returned to normal.

At least, the last I inquired, it had. If salt in the corner has any influence, it may stay this way.

THE BIG WIND OF '50

Most of us in the Valley will never forget the Big Flood of '72.

Mrs. Grace Walker of Yardley, Pennsylvania, will never forget the Big Wind of '50, as it came to be called, after that devastating December fifth when high storm winds blasted at the Valley's homes, cars, roads and rivers and left a broken path in its wake.

Grace Walker was Mrs. Arthur Pope in those days. She and her husband and children lived on Rotary Island, a small island in the Delaware River not far from Trenton, New Jersey. The place was owned by a Christian group that kept it as a vacation retreat for area members of their faith. The Popes were caretakers keeping an eye on the large Community Hall and the surrounding facilities during the off season, guarding against vandalism.

It was an island adventure for the whole family. They loved it. Getting out to the well-wooded stretch of land in the middle of the river was a Robinson Crusoe experience in itself. One had to take a raft that was tied up on the Jersey shore and pull it out to the island along a cable tow that extended from a mooring at the river's edge to a concrete base on the island shore.

Mr. Pope supplemented the family income by working the late shift at an oyster cracker factory in Trenton. He would arrive home about half-past one in the morning, pull his way across the river by the rays of a spotlight on the island guiding his way in the darkness.

On the fateful night of December 5, 1950, Grace Pope lay restless in bed. A storm that had been brewing all day was now unleashing its fury through the Valley.

When the phone rang and it was Arthur checking on them all, Grace heaved a sigh of relief.

"So glad you called, Arthur! You mustn't try to come home! The river is wild tonight. The wind has it whipping in waves all along the shore. You'd have trouble… "

Arthur broke in, "I can't stay away, Grace. Not in this. I'd worry myself sick about you and the children out there alone."

"Arthur," Grace shouted into the receiver, "You mustn't."

"Get the spotlight on, hon', I'm coming!" Then he hung up.

Grace put a robe on, a terrible fear gnawing at her heart. She checked the children. Both six-year-old Penny and two-year-old Larry were asleep, oblivious to the raging storm. She padded down to the large, empty Community Hall and switched on the spotlight which bathed the barge steps outside in a white glow.

Grace kept her gaze riveted on the cable rope that she could clearly see bobbing like a jump rope in the fury of the elements.

It wasn't long before her eyes picked up the outlines of the barge, lifting and plunging through crashing waves of water as it surged forward slowly towards the island. Watching anxiously, she distinctly made out the figure of Arthur straining against the force of the wind, pulling like mad at the tow rope. She clasped her hands and held her breath hardly able to move, frozen with fear.

Then she saw it happen, quick as a whip strike. The cable rope plucked out the rope-eye holding it to the barge and smashed it like a bowling pin square into her husband's head, sending him spinning off the raft and into the swirling black waters around him.

Grace stifled a scream and ran to the phone to call the Trenton Police and Rescue Squad. It seemed an interminable time until someone arrived. As she sat waiting, her thoughts turned back to the family tragedy only five years ago when the Pope's baby boy was lost in a fire. A fire that destroyed their Trenton home, upholstery shop and all their belongings, taking the life of their precious Jimmy.

Grace had still not gotten over that. Now as she sat waiting, and even later, as she dully realized she was being carried off the island with her two children and taken, she knew not where, her thoughts kept spinning over and over again… *She could not take any more sorrow. It could not be. Arthur must be all right.*

"Arthur will be all right!" she heard someone say. She turned her head slowly. She was riding in a car. The man next to her was a former neighbor and friend. "I'm taking you to St. Francis Hospital," he said. "But you're not to worry. The children are safe and well, and so is Arthur, I'm sure. He's a strong swimmer and an old river man. He'll be picked up before long downriver. You'll see."

Grace Pope nodded, barely aware of what was being said and done.

The next thing she knew, she was lying on the emergency table in St. Francis Hospital. She was alone, awaiting a doctor. As she lay there, her ears picked up the sound of heavy footsteps pounding down the granite corridor towards her. At first, she thought it must be the doctor; then her heart beat faster. *No! No! That was no stranger. That was Arthur coming!* She knew the heavy, well-measured steps that were Arthur's as he trudged along in his paratrooper boots! As she arose on one elbow she heard the door click open.

Then she sat up, smiling, as tears poured down her cheeks.

It was Arthur. He was dressed in his khaki army jacket with his much-used paratrooper boots neatly laced over his ankles. His wavy chestnut-toned hair fell softly over his forehead and his blue eyes looked straight at his wife.

"Oh," exclaimed Grace, "You made it! Oh Arthur, I'm so glad! I was so worried. You know you had me scared to death!"

Arthur stood beside her and smiled down at her. Grace wondered, but didn't wish to take time then to ask, how it could be he was bone dry. There wasn't a drop of moisture on his clothes.

Arthur's voice, easy-going as usual, came to her like a casual spring breeze. "Gosh, hon', I'm all right. You should know I'm always all right. Can't imagine why you'd be worried about me. I'm happy as can be. Why wouldn't I be? I'm with Jimmy and everything's wonderful!"

With that, Arthur Pope turned on his heel and went out, closing the door behind him.

Grace just stared, her heart nearly still.

... *with Jimmy! Why, Jimmy was dead!* "Oh, no!" she called out to the empty room.

Although the Delaware River was combed for subsequent days and every inch of the shoreline searched, the body of Arthur Pope was never found.

But something had been found by Grace Pope. A final calming word from her husband that no one but she could ever know about or, perhaps believe. There was peace in the message Arthur left with her. He and Jimmy were together. That thought provides a healing comfort that has stayed with Grace Walker even until this day.

WHEN JACK DEMPSEY WASN'T LOOKING

Frank Bradley of Feasterville, Pennsylvania, will always remember that the one ghost he experienced in his life (and, as such, it will always be of eminent importance) came in the year 1926. Because it appeared at the very time he, as a boy, was listening to the Dempsey-Tunney fight on the radio.

He was so absorbed in the fast blow-by-blow description rattling along the air waves, he scarcely took note that there was someone else in the room with him.

In fact, the whole ghostly performance didn't really register until it reoccurred on subsequent nights.

The Frank Bradleys had just moved into their two-story brick Folsom Street row home in Philadelphia. The fact that neighbors shook their heads as they watched the van unload the new neighbor's belongings didn't faze the family at all. They were just being eyed by curious neighbors... one had to expect that.

"But," says Frank Jr. today, "we began to realize they were expressing more than curiosity. They were being sympathetic! I remember one neighbor—his house was right next door—eased over to my father just as he was carrying in a box. With know-it-all tones, he asked my father if he was aware of what he was moving into.

"My father just kept going in and out, back and forth, but the man didn't give up. He finally came to the point.

"'That house is haunted. Everybody in the neighborhood knows that. Not one of 'em would live in it for a million bucks!'

"Dad just looked at him, gave him a nod and went on with his chores.

"'Some guy hanged himself right in that there basement! He's been haunting the place ever since!'

"My father stopped, looked back at him, pursed his lips a moment, then said, 'Thanks.' That was all. The neighbor shrugged and went back into his house."

The Folsom Street house was compact and well-built in a design that was called in those days, a "sunlight house." It meant the sun could shine in the front windows of the house and streak straight through the line of three rooms (living room; dining room; kitchen) and out the back windows.

Each of the three rooms was separated from the adjoining one by a set of doors that would slide back and forth on floor tracks. The doors were also constructed so that they could disappear into an open compartment cut into the side wall partitions. (Today this is known as a "pocket door.")

The Bradleys became accustomed to keeping the doors in the dividing partitions closed so that each room was quieter and more private.

It was getting late on that famous night in '26 when the vibrant young Tunney was putting on a blistering performance in the ring at Madison Square Garden. Dempsey was buckling for the first time in his fight history. Young Frank was all ears at the radio. Mr. Bradley was at work on a nighttime job; Mrs. Bradley was upstairs in bed. The young boy was devouring peanuts by the handful as he listened in rapt attention to the radio in the living room.

He thought he was alone.

In spite of the low din from the newscaster, Frank heard the sliding doors separating the front room from the dining room rattle along the track as they opened up. The footsteps on the wood floor creaked slowly across the room behind him and moved out into the hall and up the stairs.

Reluctantly, Frank Jr. pulled his ear away from the set over which he was hovering and glanced back at the doorway. The doors, which had been closed, were in a open position.

He then peered curiously into the hall which, by now, was empty. *Who had come through? Had Dad come home and let himself in the back way? No, it was too early.*

At that moment, the young boy heard his mother's voice floating down the stairwell.

"Is that you, Frank?"

The boy got up and went to the foot of the stairs.

His mother, with an oil lamp in hand, was staring down at him.

"Did your father come in? I heard someone coming up the stairs a minute ago and I thought it was Father, but they walked right past our bedroom and went into the middle room. I got up and checked to see what was going on. There's no one up here and you're down there… "

"I heard someone too—thought I did," said Frank. "But we musta imagined it. I've been here all along and there's no one around down here."

Mrs. Bradley returned to bed and Frank to the fight. As he later prepared for bed, he thought with wonder over the Tunney upset. But behind all that, there was a nagging question about those footsteps. Funny, he had heard something. And his mother too. *Could they both have been imagining?* Then there were the doors. He was sure they had been closed, but then he also knew he'd heard them moving across the floor track. *What was going on?*

The wonder was to increase. The next night, as Frank was again sitting up late listening to the radio, the same thing occurred. Once again, his mother appeared downstairs with the oil lamp in her hand. Together they searched the whole house, including the basement.

Finally, Mr. Bradley remained home and the whole family made a point of staying up and listening for the ghostly performance to take place. They were not disappointed. At the same hour the sound of footsteps began on the cellar stairs, proceeded upwards, until the cellar door slowly opened into the dining room. From there the footfalls creaked towards the dining room, where the separating doors slowly opened, and the steps fell clearly along the wood flooring, out into the hall and up the stairs. Once upstairs, they passed down the narrow hall and into the middle bedroom where they ceased.

No one occupied the middle room. "I guess no one wanted to after that," declares Frank today.

"So what did we do? Like everyone before us, we moved!"

Frank Bradley says the house had to be taken over by the city for some years as no one would live there. It was even condemned at one time, he recalls. However, the house still stands, neat and crisp as the day it was built with no ghosts to mess it up, either in the basement or anywhere else, according to its present tenants.

Frank enjoys a modern new home in Bucks County with nary a ghost.

As for Jack Dempsey, he never knew what happened from the Other World while he was "getting spooked" by Tunney in this one.

SHE SEES SPIRITS AT THE SEASHORE

There can be no doubt *something* is going on in one area of the Jersey seashore, whether Blackbeard combs the beaches for lost treasure or not.

That spot is Avalon. If you don't believe me, ask Mrs. Nancy Gardiner who's been living all year round in that seashore resort for almost a decade. She and her whole family have experienced chilling incidents that seem to defy explanation, unless you can accept the solution that Nancy considers to be the only possible answer: the Gardiners are haunted.

Who is the spirit? Well, Nancy feels it is a sea captain from the last century, for in the first Avalon home they occupied (which has since been moved to the north end of town) she found maritime books, naval instruments and whaling harpoons in the basement that apparently had belonged to him.

The first startling incident occurred in that captain's home when Mrs. Gardiner was standing at a bookcase looking through some old books. She felt a firm hand placed on her shoulder, as though someone were trying to get her attention and was about to speak. She looked quickly around, expecting to see her husband standing right beside her, but found no one was there. Her husband was sitting on the far side of the room, reading.

Later, as Nancy was walking past the fireplace area, she felt a distinct brushing against her lower leg as though a small animal, a cat or dog, had rubbed against her. Looking down in surprise, she saw nothing.

Startled by these rather weird incidents, Nancy nonetheless decided to make no mention of them to anyone. "They'd want to lock me up in the Looney Bin!"

But some time later, two experiences occurred which were so inexplicable, Nancy Gardiner couldn't remain quiet any longer. She was lying down in her upstairs bedroom one afternoon resting, while her youngest daughter Bobbie Jo napped, when she heard the doorknob of the closed door rattle. She looked over and saw it slowly turn.

"Is that you, Lynn?" she called out, thinking her oldest daughter must have returned early from school. There was no reply and the doorknob slowly returned to a static position. Nancy arose, opened it and peered down the steps that led to the front door below. Nothing was there.

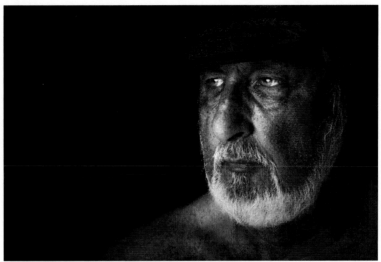

Not long after that, a similar experience occurred late one night. Nancy was reading in bed when she heard footsteps coming up the flight of steps, clear as the sound of her own footfalls on the stair treads when she would ascend them. She put down her book and waited. In a second the doorknob started turning again. Her heart began to beat faster as she called out, "Who's there?"

She received no answer, so, as before, she got up out of bed, opened the door and checked carefully all around. Her husband was away, her two older daughters, Lynn and Alana, were asleep and her baby was with her. There was no one it could be. She returned to bed, thoughtfully. Once more the brass doorknob began to rattle.

Exasperated now, Nancy Gardiner spoke out with all the patience she could muster.

"All right, Captain, if you want to come in, then come in, but stop annoying me!"

The doorknob ceased rattling immediately and it never occurred again.

Just before Christmas time of that following year, Mr. Gardiner went down into the basement. Within minutes, Nancy and Lynn who were sitting in the living room wrapping presents, heard him come charging up the stairs. It seemed he felt a presence of somebody else down there with him. Nancy smiled up at his white face. "That's just the captain. I think he lives down there with his harpoons and chests. He's just afraid you'll bother him. But he won't hurt you, I'm sure."

Not long after these disturbances, the Gardiners had to find a new home. The captain's house was to be moved to the other end of town. They found a new home and moved in, thinking that now all would be quiet. They couldn't have been more wrong.

Nancy was in the storage pantry one morning looking for some canned goods when close to her, without any warning, a beautiful gold-trimmed cake plate jumped out of a deeply-recessed cabinet shelf and onto the floor, smashing to pieces!

The incident was startling and heart-breaking. It was an heirloom piece which had belonged to her grandmother and it had meant a great deal to her.

"That was the first mean thing the captain had ever done and it made me feel very sad. He continued to be nasty," Nancy relates. "Just a few days ago, I went out one afternoon and he locked me out! Yep, I found the storm door locked when I tried to get back in! When I got in through the back door, I had no sooner swung it open than I heard three loud raps on the back of it. It wasn't my imagination, either. Bobbie Jo heard it, too!"

Nancy goes on to tell about the most recent problem. "On several occasions, both my husband and I have found the back door, which we are always careful to keep double-locked, standing wide open! That really shakes you up, you know!"

Nancy Gardiner sighs. "I don't like all this trouble-making, yet I think I understand. The captain doesn't like his house being moved. There is no basement now and he has no place to stay. The basement was his favorite place. That's why we always found the cellar so cold from his presence."

Now, Nancy's voice becomes very sympathetic.

"Perhaps, as he finds he's most welcome here, he will become less cantankerous and easier to live with."

No ghost could ask for more understanding than that.

MARILYN MONROE—
THE WORLD'S SEXIEST SPIRIT GUIDE

Kathy McGuire of Lawrenceville, New Jersey, is a very pretty blonde with sun-streaked hair, sparkling blue-green eyes, and a soft, velvety tone of voice which seems faintly reminiscent of someone else. That brilliant smile, that walk of easy abandonment... you're captivated by Kathy's feminine charms but you can't quite decide whom she brings to mind.

Then it comes! Marilyn Monroe!

This, you will see, is not surprising. Through a very unusual series of "contacts," Kathy discovered a few years ago that she had more than an inborn psychic sense directing her path in life; she had a spirit guide. A spiritual advisor who identified herself as "Norma Jeane."

The night the soft, sugary, whispering voice first spoke out to ten -year-old Kathy, the little girl thought her heart would pound itself right out of her body.

"It's me! Norma Jeane!" Young as she was, Kathy knew who that was. She well recalled the true life name of the dazzling film star, Marilyn Monroe.

Kathy squeezed tightly onto the bed covers that night as she listened with joy and excitement. Now, Kathy feels, it is not a heart-skipping moment or two; it's a natural conversation between two kindred souls.

It all began in 1959 when Kathy was visiting Hollywood. She was near the fabled Graumann's Chinese Theater where a Marilyn Monroe picture was opening for the first time. The illustrious Marilyn would be attending the show herself that evening. Kathy was only nine years old, but already she idolized the gorgeous superstar.

Kathy waited patiently at the curbside. She felt an inward tingling. Something wonderful was going to happen. She just knew it. In the next instant, a long black Cadillac drove slowly toward her and pulled to a complete stop in a binding traffic snarl. On the back seat sat a beautiful, shimmering woman. Her fair hair was full-blown and waxen-light, like the stuff that shapes Christmas tree angels. Her gown was glistening white with a low scooping neckline and her curving arms were encased in long kid gloves.

The beautiful star looked out the window and directly into Kathy's fixed gaze.

The child felt her mouth open ever so slightly and her eyes fix themselves in complete enchantment on the face of Marilyn Monroe.

As she gazed back at little Kathy, the vivid blue eyes of the actress brimmed over with moisture and tears slipped down the smooth cheeks.

Kathy was stunned. Why did the beautiful Marilyn weep when looking at her? Today, Kathy wonders still. Did the inwardly falling star see something of herself in the face of the little girl?

At that time, nine-year-old Kathy knew of nothing else to do but smile. Miss Monroe, still tear-stained, smiled back; then the touching moment was gone. The limousine moved on and Kathy never saw her dream star again.

Not in the flesh, that is.

It was a few years later, when Kathy was twelve, that one of the strangest experiences ever to occur, happened. It was in the summer of 1962. A day that was making headlines all over the world, for America's great sex symbol, who had died of an overdose of pills, was to be buried in Hollywood.

Kathy's father was sick in bed and young Kathy crawled in next to him to watch the news on television. Who wasn't watching TV that day waiting to catch a glimpse of the latest reports on the ill-fated movie queen?

As Kathy snuggled close to her father's shoulder, the young girl suddenly felt terribly ill. Her stomach was somersaulting and her head ached so violently she thought her temples would burst. She closed her burning eyes and put her hands over them. Almost immediately, she felt a sense of complete release and ease. She had the sensation of rising up off the bed and floating serenely.

Smiling with the buoyancy she now felt, the girl opened her eyes. She looked about her in stark amazement! She was no longer lying on her father's bed, she was standing in a hushed chapel-like building. She blinked her light-green eyes. Ahead of her was a casket. Lying in it, on a snowy satin tufting, was the outstretched form of Marilyn Monroe. Her fair hair was soft and framing, her face shone from its pillow of satin as beautiful as it always had from the silver screen.

Kathy walked slowly towards the still form in its dark box. There was no one else around. Only silence. Kathy leaned down and gazed into the peaceful face. Marilyn was dressed in a pale pink suit. To the young girl the color seemed sweet and delicate.

Kathy realized at that moment that her nostrils were filled with a delightful fragrance that made her feel as if she had stepped into a fantasy garden. She took note then of the baskets and vases of various blooms and vibrant greens all around her.

At the foot of the casket was a large container bursting with brilliant red roses. Kathy edged towards the bouquet and, cautiously looking around her, pulled upwards a single sweet-scented rose. She took it to the quiet-faced Marilyn and placed it in her folded hands.

Kathy sighed and stepped back. She felt a tear drop down her cheek. Then another one. A good friend was gone. Gone forever. She shut her eyes vehemently. "No! No!" she called out.

"What is the matter Kathy? Why are you shaking so and calling out like that?"

It was her father's voice. Kathy opened her eyes and found herself looking up into her father's concerned face. She was lying nestled close to his shoulder.

"You fell asleep, child. Such a sound sleep. I could not awaken you. But no matter. It was only a few minutes. And you can sit up now and watch the news. I know you'll want to see this. They're going to tell us all about Marilyn Monroe's funeral!"

In a near state of shock, Kathy pulled herself up and blinked. *What had happened? Why was she back here? How did she get to... ?*

Joe DiMaggio had just been interviewed on television. "I am puzzled," he was quoted as saying. "Who put a rose in Marilyn's hands? I had planned to do that, myself!"

No one knew the answer to that question except young Kathy McGuire, and she had something to prove it to herself for long hours afterwards. Her fingers on one hand stung from the pricking of thorns. There was even blood on them which, saying nothing, she washed off. There was an ache in her heart as she did so.

The aching didn't last long, however. Norma Jeane came to young Kathy one quiet night not long afterwards and has consistently visited her ever since.

"She is my spiritual guide and mentor," laughs Kathy with a little Monroe pursing of the lips. "When she first came to me I was really plump and Norma Jeane, in her own gentle way, let me have it. 'You'll be an ugly duckling, Kathy,' she warned 'if you don't try to make something of yourself.'"

Kathy McGuire glows like silk in candlelight when she recalls their early meetings. "Norma Jeane's voice was so very soft and gentle; so warm and full of love and caring," she recalls with a tiny shake of her head.

"Take it from me," the actress-spirit had continued, "because I know. I'm telling you now because it took me a long time before I figured it out. You can start this moment. Think about what is right for you... the most flattering clothes, the most stylish hair-do, the best make-up. I'll help you. All you have to do is listen."

And Kathy has been listening ever since. She's absorbed all the advice given to her from Norma Jeane and has never regretted it. In fact, the one time she rebelled and chose her own make-up tint, the results were disastrous. She's never strayed since from the "Monroe Method!"

"It's strange," comments Kathy, as she blinks her clear-green eyes at you, "from the time Norma Jeane came to me, I began to look like her. Actually, I'm not built like her at all, yet I'm so often told I look like her. Once I got into modeling, the likeness became very apparent. Particularly in photographs, I seem to come out looking more like Marilyn than I do Kathy McGuire!"

As for some inside information on Marilyn Monroe's demise…

"She didn't mean to kill herself," Kathy relates. "She had, in fact, just a few days before, formulated a plan for a whole new life for herself—and Norma Jeane has never lied to me."

The touching influence between the two fair-haired young women came out into the "light of day" once more. At a recent séance, the medium commented on a piece of spiritualistic knowledge.

"When you give love to someone who has passed on to the Other World and give freely, without asking for anything in return, that spirit soul will give you a spirit-rose. In fact, the passing of a spirit-rose from one soul to another is the ultimate symbol of love." With those words, the medium looked upon Kathy and said, "You have done this yourself. You have passed a spirit-rose."

Kathy just nodded.

Marilyn Monroe would like that. It's been said she resented being typecast as America's premier sex-symbol. How much better she must cherish the spiritual love symbol of the rose.

Lady in White

The Kensey John homestead was one of the busiest and happiest places in the environs of New Castle, Delaware. But on a cold winter night in the late 1800s, it was the scene of one of the strangest incidents ever to occur within its walls.

It was "visiting day" and several friends of Mrs. John's had come for mid-day dinner. One of the younger couples present had brought their baby with them, all of which was no problem, for Mrs. John owned a much-used cradle. She brought it down from the cool upstairs bedchamber and placed it by the coal stove in the parlor. The parlor stove on a blustery winter day such as this, kept the coal shuttle busy from the early morning hours on.

It was early afternoon when the snow began to fall. It dropped a fluffy white mantle over all the fields, the barn and the stately manor house. From time to time, a guest would put down her sewing and peer through a lace-curtained window, or a husband would knock the ashes out of his pipe bowl as he studied the heightening depths of snow banking against the fence outside.

Finally, Mrs. John announced that dinner was ready and the company, with a murmur of pleasure, followed her out of the parlor, across the hall and into the candle-lit dining room, sweet with the fragrance of roasted chicken and bursting hot sweet potatoes.

The young wife lingered behind a moment to tuck the hand-woven blanket tighter around the sleeping form of her baby, then with a final glance at the pine cradle, she left the parlor and joined the others, where one empty high-backed chair awaited her.

It was only shortly after the last of the steaming vegetable bowls had been passed that the young wife paused with her fork in the air. Was that crying from the parlor? She listened tensely. It was. A low murmur of a troubled fretting floated across the hallway to her ears. The husband smiled and put a restraining hand on his wife's arm.

"Don't be concerned, dear. She'll quiet down." The wife tried to return the smile and went on eating slowly. The sound grew into a sharp crying, then a fierce wailing. The wife half rose from her chair but the young husband put down his water goblet and faced her with determination. "Let's not start out parenthood designing our every movement around the whims of our child! After all, we are dinner guests. Let's act like it!"

Mrs. John wiped her lips with a corner of a linen napkin.

"Please, let me look in on the little one. It's no bo—" she started to say.

The young husband nodded, acknowledging her courtesy, but assured her that would not be necessary.

As the young mother commenced eating again, slowly and with obvious distress, the piercing screams from the parlor began to subside to a fretting and, finally, diminished to what sounded almost like a cooing of delight.

The wife relaxed and the husband reached out, patting her arm in a congratulatory gesture.

When Mrs. John arose to prepare the final touch of whipped cream on a molasses pudding, the young wife got to her feet abruptly.

"I cannot enjoy a further bite, until I see if our baby is asleep—" With these words she swept past her husband's chair and across the hall into the parlor.

In the darkening afternoon, the only lights in the brown-woodworked room were the flickering oil lamps on the mantel and a dancing light piercing the coal stove's patterned ironwork.

The wife put one hand to her high-necked blue gown and just managed to keep herself from calling out. A woman was sitting in a low chair by the baby and with one pale hand was rocking the cradle.

She was dressed completely in white, even to a pearl comb in her dark hair and milky-soft kid slippers on her slender feet. As she leaned over the baby's sleeping form, she was softly crooning. The song was somehow faintly reminiscent of a tune the wife had heard as a child herself.

The wife was about to step closer and speak to the woman when her husband swept in through the doorway. "Come, my dear—" he started, then stared at the still, bent-over form at the cradle.

"Who is—"

"I don't know," she said. Then a step forward. "Pardon me, have you just arrived? Truly, we are grateful to you for caring for our baby, but—"

The husband pushed past her and gazed carefully down at the frail form sitting by the cradle. "—not at all necessary," he concluded for his wife. "She is our responsibility, you know, not anyone else's."

The couple stood silently for a moment, waiting for a response. The fragile figure in white silk at their feet seemed utterly unaware of their presence, only watching with gentle eyes the tiny form before her.

"Come, my dears, you are missing the best pudding this side of the Mason-Dixon Line," announced Mrs. John who had breezed in through the parlor door with a rustle of silk skirts.

"Why, goodness gracious! Who is this charming lady?"

The couple turned towards her with a mystified expression. "We were just wondering, if we had retired in such haste to the dining room, we had left behind rather unceremoniously, one of your more genteel and unobtrusive guests," murmured the husband.

"Goodness gracious, no! I don't believe I have ever met the young lady, but whoever you be, my dear, you must join us at the table. If you've come to us through that world of snow, you must, indeed, be ready for a goodly roast chicken even if it is a mite less than steaming hot at this point."

Mrs. John rushed forward and with a positive reach of her arm leaned over and pulled the young woman in white to her feet. "Come, you shall sit at the table with us—and hurry and catch up so that you may enjoy some of my molasses pudding before there's not a morsel left!"

The pale guest stared as though completely surprised at the interruption, but she followed the forceful direction without a murmur. At the table, from time to time, each guest flicked a studying stare at the delicately-featured woman. None felt it was a good idea to try any conversation with her so she ate in complete silence at her place.

The young mother observed with amazement that the garments of the newly arrived guest were as pure and untouched white as the still falling snow outside the windows. There was something unearthly about her whole demeanor. She longed to share her curiosity about the woman with her husband or the hostess, but there was no opportunity to speak freely.

Nor was there for the remainder of the visit. A visit which extended through the rest of the afternoon, the long dark evening and finally, through the whole night when it became clear to all—no one would be leaving that house that night. The farm lane was impassable, as would be every road around New Castle.

Mrs. John arose to the occasion with flutter and fortitude.

"We have plenty of accommodations for all," she announced. "Come, follow me, everybody, and I will show you to your rooms."

"You my dear, seem the most weary and I shall give you the warmest and friendliest room in the house," Mrs. John said with a smile as welcoming as the coal hearth across the room. "Make yourself at home and I shall be up to awaken you at seven for a hearty breakfast!"

She was speaking to the slim, pale-gowned guest who simply followed her into the empty room and turned, closing the bedchamber door behind her without a word.

Mrs. John straightened, obviously a bit piqued for the first time. But with her head held high she started to continue down the hallway with the balance of her guests in tow, when abruptly, she reversed softly, her steps. Tiptoeing back to the first chamber she quietly turned the key in the outside lock of the door and pocketed it in her skirts.

Nobody said a word, but sensing the oddness of the situation, walked down to the far end of the hall at their hostess' suggestion.

Joining them, she whispered, "I assure you that I don't ordinarily lock my guests in their chambers, but there is something about that young woman that is certainly not ordinary. I felt it safer and more reassuring to us all to make certain that she remains in her chamber until I call her in the morning."

Everyone murmured words of agreement, though no one knew how to comment further on the obviously mysterious woman who had arrived into their midst from out of nowhere.

"Let us ask Mrs. John in the morning," suggested the young wife as she tucked her baby into the crook of her arm and sunk down into the deep feather bed, "if there has ever been a young woman living in this house who might fit the same description as the "Lady in White." Somehow, I think she belongs here. Or did belong here at some past time."

But the next morning proved too unnerving to everybody in the house for the wife to ask her questions. When the young couple appeared in the oak dining room for breakfast, only the hired girl was present, pouring thick milk into a tall pitcher.

The couple found Mrs. Kensey John in the parlor, stretched out on a red velvet sofa. She was fanning herself, in spite of the cold air in the room.

Suddenly she sat up, completely ruffled. "She's gone," she gasped out. "Gone!"

"You mean, the Lady in White?" asked the young wife.

"None other! She's completely and utterly gone! I locked the door. You saw me! There is no other key. The windows in the room are still bolted on the inside. Yet, she's not to be found anywhere. I tell you, she was not from this earth!"

"But we saw her... touched her. She ate with us," sputtered the young husband.

"I know, but all the same, she was not human! I'm sure of it!"

The rest of the guests assembled around the parlor in quiet consternation. No one could explain the strangest occurrence that probably ever took place in New Castle. As an added note of oddity, the male guests, upon checking, found not a trace of footprints in the snow outside.

Even to this century, though the eerie tale was told and retold in every parlor in the area for years and years, there has never been an answer given.

The farmhouse still stands, nestled back off of Dupont Highway. I have gazed at its worn walls and hemmed-in fields outlined heavily by modern development.

But, perhaps, nothing will hide the long ago incident of a visit to the John's farmhouse by a ghost gowned in white silk and silence.

PENNSBURY'S HAUNTED CHAMBER

Looking upon William Penn's handsome manor estate on the Delaware in Bucks County, Pennsylvania, in its reconstructed beauty one recaptures the glory it had in Penn's day. As such, Pennsbury is a soul-inspiring sight.

But step back in time for a moment and look upon the manor house as it was after the Revolution.

Spirits hover over William Penn's reconstructed 17th century country estate.

It was in ruins.

William Penn had been dead for nearly a century. His dream home, to which he had been unable to return after his last visit to America in 1700-01, just about died with him. His three sons, John, Richard and Thomas, inherited Pennsbury and tried to keep it up. But this was not easy. It was a most costly operation and not a locale particularly desirable to the sons; their interests lay far afield. The Penn boys fixed up the house, painted the wood paneling for the current day's taste, and rented out the place to a series of tenants. The rental arrangement called for upkeep of the property by the tenant, contrary to the present day custom of the owner fulfilling that responsibility. The result was practically immediate. The tenants were unable to afford the cost of upkeep for the great country estate. Pennsbury Manor began to suffer from neglect. Little by little it fell into disrepair.

The mansion was not built to survive time, as its mortar was made of lime and oyster shells, and soon decayed. As early as 1732, the building was becoming a shambles. Thomas Penn put the estate in order again, repairing and restoring it in 1735. It was useless. By the 1750s, Pennsbury was descending downhill again.

For a while during this period, two grandsons of William Penn's, both John by name, cousins to each other, (sons of Richard and Thomas) lived at Pennsbury. But like their predecessors, they were unable to cope with the length, depth and breadth of decaying Pennsbury. War was imminent. One of the Johns was detained in New Jersey shortly after the outbreak of the rebellion. It was a period of neglect for all homes in America and Pennsbury got more than its fair share. It fell into bad disrepair during and after the Revolution. By 1797, as recorded in a man's diary of that time, the great manor house was a pile of ruins.

The Penn boys disposed of the estate property by dividing up the lands into two hundred and fifty and five hundred acre portions. A family by the name of Crozier bought the land that held the mansion and surrounding houses. They lived for years in the only structure standing intact—the bake and brew house.

Eventually they decided to build larger quarters. They knocked down the mansion ruins, garden walls, etc., and buried them under five feet of dirt. On top of this ground they built a frame farmhouse which was the family homestead for many years. Years later, the family heirs sold the farm and moved to the Main Line area.

In the early 1930s, the state of Pennsylvania acquired the richly-historical site, moved the farmhouse to one side (where it serves today as the home of the director of Pennsbury) and started digging for foundations. During the reconstruction project, portions of a basement were unearthed as well as a garden wall; a few packings of green tiles (which frame three fireplaces in the mansion today) and some metal spikes used by the aristocratic families in England for the flooring (they are in place now in the entry hall floor). The rest is pure and beautiful reconstruction, following in careful detail the plans as outlined by Penn to his secretary in letters of instruction from England.

A new life for Pennsbury, worthy of its background.

But what of its fallen years? There's a kind of awe and beguiling beauty in its state of forgotten glory, too.

John Fanning Watson, the great Philadelphia antiquarian of that time, was especially intrigued by historic buildings and property. He visited them, like hundreds of other people who considered an old place in demise to be literally "a free for all." People thought nothing of carrying off bricks, lintels, pieces of ornamental carvings or plantings as souvenirs. It was a kind of accepted vandalism of the day. In his collection of relics, Watson proudly displayed a fragment of a pilaster capital from Pennsbury's front door and a piece of bed covering "curiously worked by Letitia Penn." (Letitia lived at Pennsbury and was the best-known of Penn's five daughters.)

It is an interesting fact that at Winterthur today the diary kept by Watson is preserved as well as a piece of Letitia Penn's handiwork. His famous book, *Annals of Philadelphia*, was largely based on notations made through the years in his diary.

In his book, Watson tells how Penn's manor house fell into early disrepair. A leaden reservoir on top of the house, kept for retaining water as a security against fire, began to leak. Eventually it rotted the interior and caused it to fall into "premature decay."

But is this all sadness, corrosion and decline? Not so. Not even to a devout historian like John Watson. It was also haunting and mysterious in quality. Watson describes the place at that time as "a hallowed haunt though but in ruins seen." It had, he tells us, a room—"a furnished chamber hung with fine tapestry... in which the family descendants were intended to be lodged in case of visits."

This was no ordinary room, he wrote. It was a "spirit room... a haunted chamber."

Close your eyes a moment and see the very old Pennsbury as Watson must have seen it. The moonlight washes the river with cool silver, then pours over the half-standing manor house. The stairway creaks as we mount it. On the second floor, a middle room with casement windows facing the Delaware holds its own in the forgotten falling house. The light of the white moon sifts through the leaded panes of glass and rests on a canopied bed. The spread and draperies highlighted with handiwork, stir restlessly in the night breeze coming in through a broken casement. Cobwebs criss-crossing the arms of a carved chair shudder as you walk past.

Is there a sound from the doorway behind you? Does the chair seem to move and scrape the wide plank flooring as if pulled back? Did you see the embroidered bedspread depress slightly as though some form stretched wearily out upon it?

Who has come in? Soul-loving William Penn? Efficient, respected Hannah, his second wife and partner at Pennsbury? Lovely Letitia, his daughter? One of his sons? A visiting dignitary, perhaps? An Indian chief?

Who brought the haunting to the guest chamber at Pennsbury?

The answer lies in vanished ruins of a great mansion. Or in the long-buried hearts of people who knew and loved and couldn't forget the place called "Pennsbury."

THE HITCHHIKER

For a memorable haunting experience, nothing can surpass the ghostly hitchhiker. The following story is as fine a one as I have ever come upon. It happened to two residents of Lambertville, New Jersey, who were long-time good friends.

Anne and Josie, as I shall call them, first experienced the startling phenomenon in late January of 1972. They had been to a wonderful party at a friend's house in Dublin, a village on the outskirts of Doylestown in Bucks County, and were on their way home late at night.

Anne was busy talking and reminiscing about the great time they'd just had when, right after swinging off a side road onto Route 313, she caught sight of a figure in the beam of her car headlights. It was a young man with blond hair, dressed in brown slacks and a brown jacket with a pack on his back.

As the car caught up with him, the youth turned. His shining golden hair was eye-catching in the darkness and even his eyes, as they peered into the glare, seemed bright and piercing to the women's surprised gaze.

"What in the world would anyone be out hitchhiking at this late—" started Josie, her own blue eyes wide with amazement.

"Who knows?" answered Anne with a shrug as she swerved the car around the boy, wildly gesticulating for a ride.

92

"Hey, walk it, Buddy! The fresh air is good for you!" she yelled out the window.

Josie laughed and turned the conversation back to the party and the night's good time. The car eased through the blackness with a purr. In no time they were at Easton Road in Doylestown. They stopped at the light, then pushed across the wide highway as the signal flashed in their favor.

They were no sooner across, still on Route 313, when, much to their astonished eyes, they caught sight of a figure approaching them on the far side of the road. It was clad all in brown... pants, jacket and pack on the back. The young man with the dazzling blond hair was now walking towards them!

Anne braked suddenly with the surprise, then pressed her foot down on the accelerator, spurting the car forward in the dark.

"I don't know what tricks that guy's up to but we're getting far away from him. I don't like what's going on," grumbled Anne.

"But Anne, how could he be 'up to' anything? How could anybody walking get several miles away in a few minutes? Faster than we could drive it?" asked Josie, her soft voice filled with wonderment.

"Probably had a motorcycle hidden in the bushes or something."

Josie winced at the comment, "Oh, come on, Anne! Get real! Nobody's passed us on this road since we left the party! That boy is strange. There's something odd about him. His whole weird 'brown' appearance, his bright yellow hair, even his blue eyes..."

"Blue eyes?" mumbled Anne. "How the heck do you know he has blue eyes?"

"I could just see them. Somehow, I could. They were a cold piercing blue. The kind that stare straight through you."

A long, thoughtful silence followed Josie's last remark as the two women rode homewards up York Road towards the New Hope-Lambertville bridge, over the Delaware River.

The car sped into New Hope on the moonless night. It was cold outside and the trees along York Road were crackling dry in a shaking wind. Anne braked as they approached the small bridge that spans the old New Hope canal.

Then she heard a gasp from her friend. Josie was pointing ahead.

"Look!" she exclaimed. Anne looked towards the side of the bridge they were now easing onto. There he was again! Walking, once more. He turned and signaled for a ride. They were so close to him now that they could see every feature of his countenance in the headlights. His face was thin with delicately cut bones and hollow cheeks. The sharp staring eyes seemed to stab right through Josie. Impulsively, she rolled down her window.

"Hey! Where do you want to go?" she leaned out and called as Anne stopped the car.

In the same instant, right before the eyes of both women, the figure of the young man vanished. There was nothing on the bridge with them but a cold January wind.

Anne and Josie stared at each other. It was the strangest thing that had ever happened to either one of them and they didn't know what to make of it. Many times afterwards when they would be going someplace together, they would speak of that strange night. Then finally the memory of it faded and they talked about it no more.

Until the spring of '72, when the two of them happened to spot the ghostly traveler walking the highways again late one April night. This time it occurred in New Jersey. The two friends were coming home from Flemington around midnight. They were in two different cars, Josie ahead of Anne, headed along Route 202 towards Lambertville. Just as Josie glided past the old Music Circus, she was startled to see a figure at the side of the road, going in her direction. He was dressed all in brown, as before, but without a pack on his back. It was the same young man with the blond hair and stabbing blue eyes!

Josie blinked her lights on and off and honked to signal Anne, who drew alongside of her. Both cars stopped.

"Do you see what I see?" asked Josie, tremulously.

"You bet I do!" shouted Anne. "It's time to split! Let's get the heck outta here!" With that, she shot forwards and Josie followed, fighting off cold shivers. With her heart beating fast, she forced herself to look back in the rear view mirror. He was gone. The highway in her wake was deserted.

Now the two friends think twice before driving home late at night—and who can blame them?

Top Floor Phantoms

In Malvern, Pennsylvania, stands an old brick building, worn and paint-frail, but imposing nonetheless. Built over a hundred years ago and added onto in the early years of the century, the place has seen a lot of living. For many years it served as a community building.

Finally, after this active existence, it became an apartment house with a quiet life of no fuss, frills or embellishments of beauty. Just apartments.

Unless, one wants to count the beauty of a slim young woman with long black hair who roams the upper floor in her diaphanous nightdress. Even its active days never saw anything like that!

But some residents in the old brick building, Stan and Regina Klugh for two, say they have.

The Klughs live on the top floor in a neatly-kept string of rooms that shape an apartment out of what was obviously once individual accommodations. Each room has its own door leading to the outside hallway. The Klughs keep them all shut and bolted save for the one in the back room, through which they enter the apartment.

The front room serves as their bedroom.

It must also be "home" to the spirit of a lovely young lady who, for all one knows, has reason to prefer it. Perhaps, she came there once and she comes back to visit again. Did some tragedy occur to her there? Or some unforgettable moment of happiness? No one can possibly ever know just who the raven-haired beauty is, nor why she comes back, but residents on the top floor are sure of one thing... she does return.

Regina saw her first in her bedroom one afternoon. Then Stan saw her that night. It was November of '71. He was sitting in the little kitchen within view of the bedroom a few feet away. Regina was busy feeding their young daughter, Kristin, at the kitchen table when he happened to look up. He saw a young woman with black hair cascading over her shoulder, dressed in an airy nightdress. Panels of chiffon fell gracefully around her ankles from the long flowing gown. She was rather short of height, about five-foot two. Stan will tell you how her face caught his gaze as though she were in a trance. Her pale face stared at him, "utterly expressionless," he recounts.

About a week later, Regina saw her again. She was standing in the far corner of their bedroom near to what was once the door from the hallway. After a second, she vanished. Regina says she also frequently feels "a presence" at night as she lays in bed. She even has the sensation of someone's warm breath coming against her face.

In addition to this, she has heard a ghostly voice. A child's voice. "There's no mistaking it," she tells you, "I awoke once about two o'clock in the morning to the sound of a sing-song voice calling, 'Mommy! Mommy!' Well, I looked at Kristin who was sound asleep and then I thought about other children who might be close by and realized there were none. Only a six-month-old baby across the hall which, of course, it could not possibly have been. So, I came to the conclusion it was some spirit child. Maybe some young child who belonged to the ghostly lady who visits us."

Not long after that night, Regina heard the voice again. This time it was in a teasing tone, as though the child were in a playful mood.

On another occasion, Regina reports that while she was working in the kitchen, she saw out of the corner of her eye, a figure of a woman with long dark hair standing off to one side. "I could feel her staring at me! When I turned to get a good look, she vanished."

It is interesting that on the day last November that Regina and Stan Klugh saw the apparition, a neighbor who lives on the same floor mentioned that she had seen a dark-haired woman standing in her bedroom. Just for a fleeting moment, then she disappeared. The neighbor has also heard footsteps on occasions.

"When it comes to ghosts, this apartment is a real humdinger," says Regina, laughing. "Our daughter just won't go into our bedroom. Though we've never said a word to her about ghostly visitors, she just seems to sense there is something spooky about that area and she won't go near it. Stan and I feel a cold spot, too, at the steps between the back room and the kitchen. Oh, we have a slew of real weird incidents occurring all the time. Like Stan's alarm clock. Stan found it had stopped at 4 A.M. one day and he couldn't wind it, nor would it tick. He just forgot about it and later when he picked it up, he found the clock worked perfectly. We've had no trouble since.

"Then there was the incident with my oven. I set it at the usual temperature for my roast and before long I smelled meat burning. I rushed into the kitchen and found the heat had been switched up to the highest degree!

"And, you know, the strangest thing happened with that old Philco radio cabinet you see over there." She pointed to the far wall of their living room where a radio cabinet of the 1930s vintage stood. "We got that from a man who said we were welcome to it. He didn't tell us at first how he got it.

"Well, we began to hear this wild scratching sound coming from inside the wooden frame as though some thing or some one were inside and trying to get out!

Well, Stan practically took the whole thing apart and we couldn't find any reason for those sounds. So I decided it was something from the spirits. I inquired around and discovered the man who had originally owned that radio had committed suicide!"

Whatever attracts so many phantom spirits to the Klugh's top floor apartment, one can never know. At least the residents do not seem disturbed—only curious. And perfectly willing to share them with interested readers like you.

GRANDMOTHER'S GHOST

Some of the most remarkable psychic phenomena ever to come to my attention are the experiences of a young lady in Philadelphia named Ann Flail.

The extraordinary happenings began about the time of her grandmother's last illness, in the spring of 1969.

"Both my first husband and I smelled flowers around the house all day long. We both agreed there was something funereal about the odor. Shortly after that, my grandmother died. That seemed to be the beginning of a new, strange world for me," Ann relates in her soft young voice.

She began to hear noises around the house that she'd never heard before. Footsteps crossing the attic floor overhead; doors rapping; windows slamming shut when no one was near them. One night her

husband woke up with the uneasy feeling that there was someone sitting on the edge of the bed. In the darkness he saw the distinct form of an elderly woman.

She had snow-white hair piled up on her head and she was holding a toddler on her lap. After a fleeting few seconds, the woman and child vanished back into the shadows. On another night, he looked up to see a bright light shining out of a mirror hanging on the wall. On another occasion, while driving to a night time job, Ann says her husband saw a dazzling glow appear before his eyes that was so intense it blinded him for a brief moment, nearly causing him to crash the car. There was no one else on the road.

As her eyes moisten up, Ann goes on to tell of another time when her husband walked into their living room and saw very clearly her beloved grandmother. There she was sitting in a rocker, rocking peacefully away. Her presence was palpable. He was so startled— the ghost looked so "real"—that he couldn't say a word. In the next instant, the figure faded away.

In April of '71, Ann remarried and moved into another home. But the changes made little difference to the "spirit world." In fact, the odd occurrences seemed to intensify.

Ann's good friend, Cecilia Chmielewski, can testify to that. She was present on many of the remarkable occasions; not the least of which was the time the two friends decided to hold a table-tilting séance in an attempt to contact Ann's grandmother. Appropriately, they used a three-legged table that had once belonged to the deceased grandmother. On her hand, Ann wore a ring which she had inherited from this lady.

The two friends placed a glass of holy water nearby and lit a single candle on the table beside them.

The first thing both girls noticed was a considerable drop in the temperature of the room. It got so cold, they had to fight off shivers. Cecilia raised her eyes for a moment as they sat waiting with the table resting on the floor between them. Her eyes caught sight of the doorknob to the room. It was slowly twisting. She couldn't utter a sound. Then she observed a bright glow issuing from the wall of the room facing her. She began to feel sick with tiny waves of nausea sweeping through her body.

"I think…" she started to say. Under their hands, spread on the table top, they each felt the delicate piece of furniture commence to pulsate. "It was as though it came to life," Ann recalls. "In the next instant, it began to lift off the floor! Truly, neither of us did anything but lightly rest our hands, palms down, on the wood surface. It was startling; it was so clearly my grandmother's presence."

It was then Ann looked over at a picture of her grandfather. A light was glowing out from the features as though spotlighted by some Other World illumination. Meanwhile, she noticed the flame from the candle was growing larger and more brilliant. The table, by now, was rocking violently back and forth.

At that moment, Cecilia cried out that some heavy weight was pressing on her shoulders. But Ann could not answer her. She was transfixed by a sight she saw clearly in front of her. Reaching down onto the table top was a fifth hand!

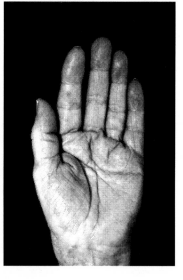

It was small and white and, gently, it pressed its palm down on the table right between theirs! Impulsively, Ann reached out to touch it. At the same time, Cecilia grabbed the candle and brought it over to the table. With that, a sudden waft of air swept across them, blowing out the flame. Then Cecilia felt the candle knocked right out of her grasp by an invisible force. Hot wax spewed all over her and the wall next to her.

The two girls leaped to their feet in shock.

The table stopped its movements; the air grew warmer; the walls and the photograph assumed a normal aspect. There was only the quick breathing of the two girls for a long time. Until Ann, looking down at the table top again, screamed out, "Look!"

On the smooth waxen surface were clearly defined the sweat imprints of five hands! Ann stared at the impression in the middle of the table. It was small and dainty. "Exactly the size of grandmother's hand!" she exclaimed.

Later on, Ann took a polishing cloth to clear away the marks from the old table top. Her imprints and those of Cecilia wiped perfectly away, but the impression the "spirit hand" remained in the middle of the table. According to Ann, she was never able to remove the mysterious handprint.

Equally startling to the two friends was the discovery of a similar phenomenon on an old buffet of Ann's which had belonged to her mother. A series of marks had been scratched into the surface of the wood, deeply carved into the grain as though a sharp-pointed instrument had been used. Only the letter "s" was actually intelligible. "It's interesting to note that my grandmother's name was 'Isabella.' The first accent of her name is definitely an 's' sound. Perhaps, she was trying to write her name so that I would know for sure it was she who was here?"

Ann goes on to tell about another inexplicable incident which she believes was a demonstration of true grandmotherly love. Recently she went into her baby's room to change his diaper, and much to her astonishment, the diaper had already been changed! A clean one had been put on and the old one lay on top of her bureau. And still more fantastic, her son's pajamas had been replaced. He was in a fresh outfit!

"And do you know?" concludes Ann Flail, "I haven't yet located the pajamas I had on him when I put him down. They just vanished!"

So ends the tale of one of the strangest hauntings that ever came to the Delaware Valley.

I See Dead People

During the Victorian era, it became a common practice to take photographs of the dead. Since these days we take pictures to celebrate life, this seems like such a sad and macabre practice. To the Victorians, however, post-mortem photography was a popular custom and when you think about it, you can probably understand why.

In the late 1800s, most families never got around to getting to a photographic studio and when a member passed on, especially if it was a sudden death, they realized they had no photograph of their loved one. They would then take the corpse to a photographic studio that specialized in photographing the dead. They believed these *memento mori* photographs marked the beginning of their loved one's ascension into eternity. The photo would also serve as a reminder of their loved one until the day that they would meet once again in heaven.

Many, many years ago one of these post-mortem photographic studios existed in Lambertville, New Jersey. It was located above the People's General Store on 28 North Union Street. I once had the opportunity to visit the studio. The old large room was still there. In it was a big upholstered chair, obviously well-used, with stuffing broken out here and there. Later I learned that the chair was the photographer's main prop for photographing his dead subjects. He would put them into this chair and shoot away with his camera. Apparently, people were very satisfied with the results. I know in my family such a photograph exits. It had a kind of fascinating terror for me as a child. As I gazed at my ancestor's face looking straight out at me, my mother would say, "She was dead when that picture was taken." I was quite impressed and a little frightened, but one thing's for sure—I never forget that ancestor's picture!

Two young men I know once had an experience that they will never forget. They decided to spend the night in the old post-mortem studio. As you can imagine, it is a large, empty, cold loft room. One of them sat on a straight chair and the other one sat in the "Chair of the Dead," as I call it. At first they were only aware of the tremendous quiet and cold. But as they sat there talking, all of a sudden in the stillness, the one in the straight chair began to feel a shower of material falling down over his head. It seemed to come out of nowhere. He and the other young man got up and looked around. They found four photographs of different sizes; old, crinkled parchment pictures. Some were bent; some curled. The one he gave me is torn and quite bent, but you can see they are pictures of old-fashioned subjects. They seemed to materialize out of thin air.

In daylight, the young men conducted a thorough investigation of the room. They looked high and low. There was no hole in the ceiling, no storage shelf, or anything they could find that might provide a proper explanation for the manifestation of the pictures. This seemed to me to be one of those strange incidents of materialization (matter appearing out of nothing).

Not long after this incident the room was rented to another occupant. I was told that the loft has been transformed into a ballet studio. The room is now filled with music and movement. The old horsehair "Chair of the Dead" is long gone... but not the memory of what once took place in that room over a century ago.

MURDER OVER AND OVER

Young Victor Barger, packing-box in hand, made his way down the creaking cellar stairs. Moving into a new home in the Frankford area of Philadelphia was exciting, even when it was an old house like this. But this time, though Victor didn't quite know why, it was frightening, too.

He fought off a shiver and stepped down. Suddenly, a cold wind swept out of nowhere and surrounded his body. He was about to call out to his father, who was close upon his heels, that a basement window must have been left open, when he stopped—he couldn't speak!

A rope, dangling from a beam above the bottom step, was swaying violently in the current of icy air. It was frayed and worn and tied into a loop at one end. It wrenched and twisted in the breeze like a "thing" alive.

With his mouth open, Victor stared. Finally, he was able to speak.

"Oh my gosh! What is it?"

His father behind him was quiet for a moment. Then he put a firm hand on the boy's back and bellowed.

"What is it? What is it? Always so curious about things you have no business with! Now put that box down in the corner; close that cellar window and get back up to your mother. There's plenty of work for an eight-year-old boy to do, without wasting time asking foolish questions!"

That night, just before bedtime, Victor took a quick peek down the cellar steps. The rope was gone.

Later, in the big bed in the back chamber of the second floor, there was finally time for Victor to ask his questions. His brother, Charlie, and a friend, Billy, lay one on either side of him.

"You lucky stiff!" groaned ten-year-old Billy. "You saw a noose! Wish I could have seen it—a real-life noose! Gee, they hang people with 'em in jails!"

"Out West," added twelve-year-old Charlie, "they hang robbers and gunmen with 'em—sometimes from a tree limb on a buryin' hill. Pirates have been hung by a noose made out of chains!"

"Boy, oh boy, wish I could have seen it!" were the last words Victor heard drifting to him from Billy's side of the bed. Then, in spite of his shivers of apprehension, Victor fell asleep.

The next day, those shivers were to grow into cold slithering feelings up and down his back when he stopped alongside the back lot of the old movie theater. Some boys were shooting marbles, but Charlie and Billy weren't. They were leaning against the theater's brick wall, talking to some older boys dressed in dirty sneakers and frayed caps and sweaters.

Billy was talking. "Geez! Did he strangle her?"

"Beat her on the head with a club?" asked Charlie.

"Naw," answered one, "stabbed her with a kitchen knife!" He turned, saw Victor and spit into the dirt.

Billy looked over at the young boy, one hand on his hip in disgust. "What do you want, Vic? Get a move on it, will ya?"

Victor couldn't speak for a moment. His stomach felt a little sick. "I'm going to the tobacco shop for Papa," he finally managed to say.

"Well then, on with it and don't be forever hanging around us, snooping into our business," snapped out Billy with impatience.

"Wait a minute, Billy," said Charlie, "how's about your errand? You're supposed to be fetching milk for your mother and I don't see a doggoned thing in that pail you're carrying but a lot of hot air!" With that, Charlie smiled and gave Billy a firm push on the shoulder blades.

The last thing Victor saw, was Billy swinging reluctantly down towards the dairy and Charlie waving goodbye to the big boys, as he turned into the pungent, invitingly warm air of the tobacco shop.

When he got home, Victor plunked the change on the kitchen table and stuck the cigars into the old humidor box in the cabinet. Mama and Papa were in the front room setting up shop. Papa's business in old gold, silver, pewter and false teeth was an easy store to pack up and move. Every time the rents went up and they had to head for another home, the old shop went along as easily as Mama's china and linens.

Victor wandered to the foot of the stairs leading up the second floor. He heard soft sounds from the back bedroom sifting down the steps towards him. Was it voices or was it little yelpings from Lady and her new brood of puppies?

Victor took the steps two at a time and hurried into his bedroom where he'd put the dog's box. He smiled. Lady was licking her cream-colored, soft-furred puppies with proper motherly concern and all was well.

The droning sounds were louder now, but still indistinct. They came from the bathroom which adjoined his bedroom at the far end, just beyond the fire escape window. The door was closed tight.

Victor edged over to it, listening carefully. The voices got louder.

Finally he heard very clearly, "She was taking a bath. They say the tub is discolored from blood stains, not rust." It was Charlie's voice.

Victor turned the doorknob and pushed open the door. The two boys were standing over the bathtub, staring into it.

Again the twisting, pinching fingers of cold cut into him as Victor formed words slowly.

"What are you looking for?" he asked, dreading an answer.

Billy straightened up. "We're not looking for anything; we're looking at something!"

"What?" asked Victor simply.

"The bathtub, stupid!" pronounced Billy.

Victor stopped at the foot of the tub, next to Charlie.

It was a gloomy-looking thing—a large wooden case that was lined with a black-stained, gray metal. It looked more like a burying box than a bathtub.

"It's the old-fashioned kind of bathtub, Victor," explained Charlie. "They used to build a big wooden box, then line it with zinc and that was your bathtub!"

It was so high, Victor wondered if he'd be able to climb into it by himself. He'd soon know, for come Saturday night in the Barger family, everybody got their weekly bath—no ifs, ands, or buts about it. Mama would pour hot water from her big copper kettle until every window nearby was steamed up.

Charlie and Billy turned on their heels and pushed back into the bedroom, leaving Victor staring at the gray metal that was stained with curious pools and streams of an almost black-red color.

"That's where it happened," Charlie was saying from the next room.

"Stabbed her; then held her down in the water? Boy, there must have been plenty of deep, red water that night in the old tub!"

"Keep your voice down, Billy," warned Charlie.

"Why? Your Mama and Papa are knee-deep in gold teeth and old silver at this point. What could they hear?"

"I'm not thinking of them," Charlie murmured.

Victor stood in the bathroom doorway. He was nearly transfixed by the conversation he was overhearing.

"What, him?" guffawed Billy. "Why are you always worrying about that kid? He's too stupid to know what we're talking about!"

"I'm not stupid and I want to know what you're talking about," said Victor emphatically.

"Well, then," boomed out Billy, "here it is! The people who lived here before you ran a laundry downstairs and didn't have nothin' more to show for it than pennies and arguments that made the walls shake. So one night the husband went cuckoo and while his wife was taking a bath, he went for the kitchen butcher knife and then walked right into the bathroom and stabbed her three times. Then he held her down till she drowned! After that, he marched down to the cellar and hung himself. He hung there till he was blue and stiff and they couldn't bend him to carry him up the stairs. They had to shove him up the stairwell like a board! Then everybody just left everything like it was... blood in the bathtub and the crazy noose still hanging there for the whole blasted three years, until you moved in yesterday. You happened to see it on account of you're so stinkin' lucky! Does all this information satisfy you? Heard enough...?"

Billy's voice stopped abruptly as Charlie swept him back against the bedroom wall with a shove.

"You talk too much, Billy! Someone should stop your mouth in the bathtub!"

Billy squirmed free of Charlie's grasp. "Who wants to say anything to that kid, anyhow? Look at his pink eyes and his white hair! He's a goon!"

Charlie twisted Billy's collar in his hands fiercely, then gritted out his words—"Don't you make fun of him, Billy. You remember what my Mama says. An albino is a special kid. You should be sympathetic to him, not picking on him!"

Victor felt a sting in the back of his eyes but he didn't cry.

"I am special," he said softly. "I can see in the dark. I can feel things you can't, because you're like everybody else!"

"That's right, Victor," said Charlie, patting him on the shoulder.

That one warm movement was too much. Victor pushed past the boys, fled downstairs and out into the alley next door. No one found him there, except soft, cool-nosed Lady who poked her head under his arm and licked his face.

That night Victor slept on the far side of the bed, Charlie

volunteered to sleep in the middle and Billy, who seemed a permanent guest, was on the other side.

There wasn't a sound for a long time except the distant chiming of the little shelf clock in Papa's shop downstairs. Victor heard it tinkle out ten notes; then later, eleven; and finally twelve. Except for him, everyone and everything in that house seemed sunk into a sleep as soft and soundless as the comforter of down resting over him.

Exactly what time it was when he heard the noise, he didn't know. There wasn't a sound from the street below, not so much as a creak from a peddler's cart wheel or a faint clatter of horses' hooves on cobblestones. Just intense quiet and then this faint sound that, perhaps, thought Victor, wasn't a sound at all, but a feeling inside his body.

He turned over on his back and listened. He could make out the soft breathing of the other two boys beside him and he could hear tiny gurgling sounds from the dog's box. He lifted his head slightly off of his pillow and looked around.

Victor almost let out a gasp as his eyes caught sight of the bedroom door handle. The shining brass knob was turning ever so slowly. So slowly, you could not be sure at first that it was turning. Then Victor watched it settle into position and heard a click as the door swung eerily open with only the slightest of creaks.

Victor strained to see across the dark room. A man stood in the open doorway. The boy could see him distinctly. He was a big, broad-shouldered man, as huge as the men who moved furniture. Unlike Victor's father, he was clean-shaven. His cheeks now looked flushed as though he were very angry. The big form took a step into the room. Immediately his figure was surrounded with a faintly glowing mist that pulsated about him as he moved. At that same moment, Victor felt cold air rush into the room as though someone had left the front door open at the foot of the stairs.

Shivering cold wracked Victor's insides with deep, twisting pain. His lips stuck together with dryness and he could not call out or even move so much as a hand towards the sleeping form of his brother next to him.

The man reached the foot of the bed, passing close by the dog's box. Victor was vaguely aware of his pet's whining and the gurgling, yelping of the puppies. The man moved on, coming around the bed on the far side of the room. Frozen with terror, Victor stared up at him.

He passed, his huge form silhouetting against the fire escape window then moved on, towards the bathroom door. The man was dressed in a long rubber apron that hung to his knees. In one hand he carried a kerosene lamp, in the other, a large butcher knife gleamed like new silver.

Oh, my Lord in Heaven, thought Victor, *he's going to that bathtub! He's going to kill his wife! Oh, Lord in Heaven, stop him! Stop him!*

Before he knew what had happened, Victor leaped out of bed and was standing, shivering, in the open doorway of the bathroom, staring into the dark interior. The bathroom was alive with dancing yellow flames from the kerosene lamp, now resting on the rickety bath stool.

"Don't do it!" he wanted to call out, but he couldn't utter a sound. The mist had enveloped him like a glimmering spider web of stickiness from which he knew he couldn't escape. In the deep interior of the fog, he could see the scene taking place as clearly as a movie in a nickelodeon.

The fleshy form of a big woman was writhing in the bathtub, sending out stirred waves as she lurched and heaved in the deep water. The man was bent over her, his hand stabbing up and down in sharp motions, and the knife in his hand gleaming redder and redder in the wan lamplight.

The woman's shrieks were piercing at first, cutting through the silence like a wild animal's. Then they slowly became muffled as the big man's hands pressed harder and harder on her chest and her tortured face began to disappear into the crimson water.

The last thing Victor saw was one white arm shoot up from the red splashing of the tub water in a final defense. It caught a slice from the knife, sending spurts of blood high against the man's face and over the wall behind the tub.

Now nothing… no struggling… no splashing… no tell-tale waves of violence. Only the soft dripping of splattered water— drip-drop, drip-drop—down off the edge of the brown bathtub and onto the sodden wooded floor.

The man turned, picked up the sputtering lamp and started for the door. His apron was oozing with blood. Quickly, Victor flattened himself against the tiny area of wall between the bathroom door and the fire escape window. The tightness of his chest choked off his breathing until he thought he would die where he stood. As the man passed by him, the icy white mist touched and swirled around Victor's face and hands until he felt numb.

Dripping with cold sweat, he stared after the moving form, watching it pass around the bed and out the door into the hall. Slowly the door closed and the shining brass knob curled back into position and was still. The mist vanished with the figure and nothing was left in the room but the stinging odor of laundry soap, the big dark bars that Mama used in her wash.

Now Victor felt his stomach relax. With sickening gasps, he put his two hands to his temples and let out the loudest shrieks his lungs could muster.

Charlie and Billy sat bolt upright as though shaken by an earthquake. The bedroom door shot open and Mama and Papa were crowding towards him. For long moments, Victor just trembled and yelled. He could make no words come out. He was only vaguely aware that Papa had turned up the gas jet and was staring at the dog's box in the corner.

Soon, Mama followed his gaze. Then the two older boys and finally, shaking with still-clinging terror, Victor edged towards the box. When he saw the dead, twisted form of the cream-colored dog surrounded by her brood of lifeless puppies, he burst into uncontrollable cries of anguish. He didn't stop sobbing for the rest of the night, even though he spent those hours close beside his mother in her bed.

The next morning the older boys looked strangely at Victor, but said nothing. Mama and Papa must have had a hand in that, decided the young boy, and he was grateful. He wanted only to forget that night. It had been far worse a nightmare than any tales he'd ever heard about Wild West gunmen and fierce-fighting pirates.

That day there was no teasing from Billy and there were extra pats on the back from Charlie, one including an invitation to join the fellows in back of the movie theater and shoot marbles.

The day flew by and Victor went to bed that night glowing with the pleasure he'd had playing with his brother and the big boys on the block.

"Now get right to sleep!" were the last words from Charlie as he turned over on his side, facing Victor and with his back to Billy. In seconds, both older boys were asleep.

Victor sighed and closed his eyes.

Then it happened again. Just as the night before.

Victor pulled himself up on one elbow. He found his ears straining to that same indistinct signal from the depths of the house. Once more, that shiver of sounds trilled through the very keyhole of the door to his waiting ears.

As before, the doorknob turned slowly and the door creaked open, sending a mist into the room that glowed from the yellow light of a kerosene lamp.

It was he. Once again, bearing the light and carrying the large, gleaming knife.

With one desperate movement, Victor clapped his hands over his ears. But nothing could keep out the thrashing noises from the deep water and the shrill cries that froze his spine.

After a few minutes, the man slipped past again and went out of the bedroom, closing the door and leaving behind him the same stomach-turning odor of heavy laundry soap.

Shivering until his bones felt they were knit into one hard lump, Victor lay back in bed in the darkness and cried until he fell asleep from sheer exhaustion.

And so it went every night for three months. Continuously, Victor saw the man come in the night. His eyes would pick out his form in the dark, his rubber apron gleaming in the lamp light; the knife aglow with its shimmering blade.

Then, one day, as abruptly as the whole thing had started, it ended. Victor found the nights uninterrupted. Peace came to the old frame house.

Other changes came about, too. When Victor was about eleven years old, his white hair turned to yellow and his pink eyes changed into a soft blue. The unusual boy of the Frankford area of Philadelphia in those early years of the 1900s was now no different than any other boy.

He liked it that way. And least of all, did he miss the knack of seeing in the dark or ever experiencing again the reenactment of that murder.

When I met Victor Barger a few years ago, he was sixty-three years old, hale and hearty, with no further memories but happy ones.

BIRDS OF ILL OMEN

Since the beginning of time, birds have been regarded with awe by mortals. Perhaps because man so envied the flight of the winged creatures, he considered the ability to rise into the heavens a divinely bestowed talent. From there he developed an association between birds and the gods. The feathered creatures were either a god come to earth in another form, or a message from the deity.

Related to this widespread belief came a natural follow-up; a bird could serve as an oracle or guide. And, they were so considered by the ancient Greeks and Romans. The practice of augury relied heavily upon birds—their actions, their flight, their songs, their coloring and so forth.

Such beliefs still exist in the world today. In American superstition, a hawk seen flying to one's left is an unlucky omen. Calls of birds with a sinister association such as the owl, are considered fearful portends. Of course, any birds that are black, such as the crow or raven, come naturally into a connection with evil or black witchcraft.

A snow white bird, by reason of its rare and eerie pureness, is regarded, especially in Great Britain and the United States, as a sign of death. In such dire roles assigned to them, the latter birds of either pure black or snow white have been labeled, "Birds of Ill Omen."

Tales of such deadly birds abound in the British Isles. Sometimes the birds are actual creatures; sometimes they are phantoms.

One story I have heard concerns a woman who was visiting friends in the Midlands of England during the last century. One night the guest was awakened by a noise in the room, as though somebody were rummaging about. She thought it must be a burglar. Horrified, she crept low under the bedclothes, scarcely permitting herself to breathe. When nothing happened, she slowly sat up and looked about her in the dense blackness. She could hear very distinctly the sound of flapping wings. Apparently, a bird had gotten into her room and was fluttering about her bed.

Much relieved, the woman arose, lit a candle by her bedside and searching around, discovered a large bird perched on top of the wardrobe. Something about its ruffled plumage struck her as eerie, but she brushed the feeling aside and proceeded to urge the creature from its perch and out the open window. It refused to comply, but kept fluttering about the room from chair, to chest, to wardrobe. Finally, it flew into a large cupboard in the wall that happened to be open. Quickly, she shut the cupboard door, and after closing the window, climbed back into bed.

At breakfast the next morning, the guest announced to her hosts what had occurred and asked their help in disposing of the bird. The family members answered not a word and went on eating.

Upon returning to her bedroom, the guest looked for her prisoner from the night before and found, to her amazement, the cupboard was empty. How could that be? There was no way that bird could have escaped!

Later, she was told by her hostess that no one at the table had dared comment on the incident, for the family's death-omen was just such a bird. They were afraid. A few days later, the visitor learned her host had received word that a brother, whom he had not seen in years, had died suddenly.

In America a similar pattern exists in the superstition that if a white bird appears on one's window sill, it portends death to someone in the household. Not quite a hundred years ago in Bucks County, Pennsylvania, the following incident was reported:

Around midnight, as a woman sat reading by the bedside of her ailing neighbor, her attention was attracted to the window by a tapping sound on the window pane. She looked up to catch sight of a snow white bird perched on the sill.

In horror, she ran to the master of the house. When he returned with her to the bedroom, his wife was dead.

Such stories, however, are not to be found only in the dim past. Mrs. J. Allyson of Philadelphia, recounted to me a chilling experience of hers that occurred when she was ten years old.

Her little brother was ill in bed. She and the rest of the family were seated around the dining room table eating, when suddenly, a whirring sound from a large bird flying low over their heads, startled them all. They put down their knives and forks and looked about them, perplexed and frightened.

There was nothing visible to be seen. Only the eerie sound of flapping wings swishing and swooping through the silence.

The young girl looked questioningly at her father. He answered her with a silent stare. Then, as the noise subsided, they all went slowly back to eating.

"None of us ever said anything, but I think we all knew," says Mrs. Allyson today. "At least, I know I understood the message, and I'm sure my father did also. It was a portend that my little brother would not recover. He died the following morning."

So birds with ominous significations do not seem to have died and gone to the Never Never Land of all featured creatures; they seem to fly on and on. They flap their threatening wings through many centuries and many lands. And sometimes... they are heard.

THE QUOTABLE SPIRIT

The supernatural world is a country where we "see through a glass darkly." We walk along its hidden ways and byways uncertain of direction but propelled forwards by a never-waning curiosity. The maps we must follow are scanty and incomplete. Therefore it behooves us to listen well to every traveler who has pondered the mysteries of this unseen, unknown, but hauntingly beautiful territory. The journey can be intriguing, baffling, astounding, exhilarating and perhaps, even terrifying at times. But for those sojourners with an open heart, a willing spirit and a questioning mind... the journey goes on and on.

Since we must understand whether ghosts and spirits exist or not, how can we find out? The way to find out whether anything exists or not is to depend on the testimony of the ears and eyes of the multitude. If some have heard it or some have seen it then we have to say it exits. If no one has heard it and no one has seen it then we have to say it does not exist. If from antiquity to the present, and since the beginning of man, there are men who have see the bodies of ghosts and spirits and heard their voices, how can we say that they do not exist?

*

MO TZU
CHINESE PHILOSOPHER ~ 470-391 B.C.

It is wonderful that five thousand years have now elapsed since the creation of the world, and still it is undecided whether or not there has ever been an instance of the spirit of any person appearing after death. All argument is against it; but all belief is for it.

*

SAMUEL JOHNSON

Where are the dead? Those who have loved us and whom we have loved. Are they gone from us forever, or do they return? Are they still among us, possessed of a mysterious and awful existence? Are there among the dead those whose love can still protect our weakness? Are there those whose troubled spirits are permitted to disturb our peace so that they can avenge their wrongs?

Between this world and that other which escapes our senses, one thing seems to be clear: we can neither explain a connecting link nor admit an impossible barrier.

This also seems certain: we are all, even the least impressionable, at times aware of things invisible. All of us, at some point or another, have experienced undefinable fear... a sense that out of the darkness that surrounds us, hidden powers lurk that may suddenly reveal themselves and throw us face to face against the unknown possibilities of the Unseen World.

*

LORD FAIRFAX
BRITISH AMBASSADOR TO THE U.S. ~ 1941-46

There is something beyond the grave; death does not end all, and the pale ghost escapes from the vanquished pyre.

*

SEXTUS PROPERTIUS

Everyone is in truth a ghost, continually passing through the physical plane, constantly materializing and vanishing in the blink of an eye, performing specific tasks as part of a universal blueprint; playing scripted roles on ghostly celluloid, using the art of illusion to dramatize and evoke emotion, oftentimes dying traumatically to enhance the drama. Nothing ever dies, for the soul is pure energy which cannot be created or destroyed, only transformed. Therefore, everyone continually lives in the dreams and memories of others, and in the collective unconsciousness of the Divine, continuing from beyond the so-called grave to learn and teach on its journey toward perfection and oneness with all things.

*

ST. GERMAIN

*Though thou seest me not pass by, Thou shalt feel me
with thine eye as a thing that, though unseen,
Must be near thee, and hath been; And when in that
secret dread, Thou hast turned around thy head, Thou
shalt marvel I am not as thy shadow on the spot,
And the power which thou dost feel... Shall be what
thou must conceal.*

*

LORD BYRON

*Ghosts are a metaphor for memory and remembrance and metaphorically
connect our world to the world we cannot know about.*

*

LESLIE WHAT

In most of the relations of ghosts, they are supposed to be mere aerial beings without substance, who can pass through walls and other solid bodies at pleasure... The usual time for their appearance is midnight, seldom before it is dark, and no ghosts can appear on Christmas Eve. If during the time of an apparition, there is a lighted candle in the room, it will burn extremely blue: the coming of a spirit is announced some time before its appearance, by a variety of loud and dreadful noises, and is rarely visible to more than one person, although there are several in company... A ghost has not the power to speak until it has first been spoken to; so that notwithstanding the urgency of the business on which it may have come, every thing must stand still till the person visited can find sufficient courage to speak to it.

*

HOWELL'S CAMBRIAN SUPERSTITIONS ~ 1831

The boundaries which divide life from death are at best shadowy and vague. Who shall say where one ends and the other begins?

*

EDGAR ALLEN POE

Millions of spiritual creatures walk the earth Unseen, both when we wake, and when we sleep.

*

JOHN MILTON

From ghoulies and ghosties And long-legged beasties And things that go bump in the night— Good Lord, deliver us!

*

SCOTTISH PRAYER

We should not pretend to understand the world only by the intellect.
The judgment of the intellect is only part of the truth.

*

CARL JUNG

Where'er we tread 'tis haunted, holy ground.

*

LORD BRYON

I think that one should accept ghosts very much as one accepts fire—a common
but equally mysterious phenomenon. What is fire? It is not really an element, not
a principle of motion, not a living creature—not even a disease though a house
can catch it from its neighbors. It is an event rather than a thing or a creature.
Ghosts, similarly, seem to be events rather than things or creatures.

*

ROBERT GRAVES ~ ENGLISH POET

The most beautiful thing we can experience is the mysterious. It is the source of all
true art and all science. He to whom this emotion is a stranger, who can no longer
pause and wonder and stand rapt in awe, is as good as dead: his eyes are closed.

*

ALBERT EINSTEIN

There are three classes of people.
Those who see.
Those who see when they are shown.
Those who do not see.

*

LEONARDO DA VINCI

Strange, that from lovely dreamings of the dead
I shall come back to you, who hurt me most.
You may not feel my hand upon your head,
I'll be so new and inexpert a ghost.
Perhaps you will not know that I am near—
And that will break my ghostly heart, my dear.

*

DOROTHY PARKER

It is all very well for you who have never seen a ghost to talk as you do,
but had you seen what I have witnessed, you would hold a different opinion.

*

WILLIAM THACKERAY

There is a fatality, a feeling so irresistible and inevitable that it has the force of
doom, which almost invariably compels human beings to linger around and haunt,
ghostlike, the spot where some great and marked event has given the color to their
lifetime; and still the more irresistibly, the darker the tinge that saddens it.

*

NATHANIEL HAWTHORNE

Forms change and pass; bodies disappear; but spirits linger, to consecrate ground
for the vision-place of souls. And reverent men and women from afar, and
generations that know us not and that we know not of, heart-drawn to see where
and by whom great things were suffered and done for them, shall come to this
deathless field, to ponder and dream, and lo! The shadow of a mighty presence
shall wrap them in its bosom, and the power of the vision pass into their souls.

*

JOSEPH LAWRENCE CHAMBERLAIN
GETTYSBURG, OCTOBER 3, 1886

Whatsoever that be within us that feels, thinks, desires and animates is something celestial and divine and consequently imperishable.

*

ARISTOTLE

It is the secret of the world that all things subsist and do not die, but retire a little from sight and afterwards return again. Nothing is dead. People feign themselves dead, and endure mock funerals and mournful obituaries, and there they stand, looking out the window, sound and well in some new disguise.

*

RALPH WALDO EMERSON

But what happens on earth is only the beginning.

*

MITCH ALBOM

This World is not Conclusion,
A sequel stands beyond—
Invisible, as Music—
But positive, as Sound.

*

EMILY DICKINSON

As soon as man does not take his existence for granted,
but beholds it as something unfathomably mysterious,
thought begins.

*

ALBERT SCHWEITZER

As a Catholic sacristan, I have been conducting funeral services for many years. Although I rarely see a discarnate spirit, I do hear them and sense the force of their personality which has survived the death of the physical body. Sometimes I may even feel an arm around my shoulder. If it is a particularly strong presence, they may try to communicate in which case I will hear them as another voice in my head. These are not my own thoughts. The tone of the voice is quite distinct from my own. They tell me they feel more alive than they did in life. I suspect it stems from the relief of having been unburdened from their earthly responsibilities and fears and the sense that they are now free from the constraints of the physical body. I've been presiding over funeral services for over fifty years and I can truly say that I have never sensed a spirit that appeared to be disturbed.

*

TINA HAMILTON
ST. THOMAS CHURCH ~ CANTERBURY, ENGLAND

The immortality of the soul is demonstrated by many proofs.

*

PLATO

Be sure that it is not you that is mortal, but only your body. For the man whom your outward form reveals is not yourself; the spirit is the true self, not the physical figure which can be pointed out by your finger.

*

CICERO

Men of broader intellect know there is no sharp distinction between the real and the unreal.

*

H. P. LOVECRAFT

Wisdom begins in wonder.

*

SOCRATES

The supernatural is the natural not yet understood.

*

ELBERT HUBBARD

Whatever else a "ghost" may be it is probably the most complex phenomenon in nature... Instead of describing a "ghost" as a dead person permitted to communicating with the living let us define it as a manifestation of persistent personal energy.

*

FREDERICK MYERS

Somewhere, something incredible is waiting to be known.

*

CARL SAGAN

For my own part, I am apt to join in the opinion with those who believe that all the regions of Nature swarm with spirits, and that we have multitudes of spectators on all our actions when we think ourselves most alone.

*

JOSEPH ADDISON

All is mystery; but he is a slave who will not struggle to penetrate the dark veil.

*

BENJAMIN DISRAELI

The ultimate gift of a conscious life is the sense of mystery that encompasses it.
*
LEWIS MUMFORD

In the right light, at the right time, everything is extraordinary.
*
AARON ROSE

There are no mistakes, no coincidences.
All events are lessons given to us to learn from.
*
ELIZABETH KUBLER-ROSS

The important thing is not to stop questioning.
Curiosity has its own reason for existing.
One cannot help but be in awe when he contemplates
the mysteries of eternity, of life, of the marvelous structure of reality.
It is enough if one tries merely to comprehend a little of the mystery every day.
Never lose a holy curiosity.
*
ALBERT EINSTEIN

Without mysteries, life would be very dull indeed.
*
CHARLES DE LINT

The big question is whether you are going to be able to say yes to your adventure.

*

JOSEPH CAMPBELL

Now about those ghosts.
I'm sure they're here (in the White House)
and I'm not half so alarmed at meeting up with any of them
as I am at having to meet the live nuts I have to see every day.

*

BESS TRUMAN
FIRST LADY 1945-1953

The world of the five senses is a world of illusion.
The most solid-looking brick is mostly empty space.
The reality of human existence has dimensions unseeable with the physical eye.

*

ARTHUR FORD

In the law of physics, energy cannot be created or destroyed,
only transferred from one form to another form.

*

LAW OF CONSERVATION OF ENERGY

It's no longer a matter of believing or disbelieving;
it's a matter of being aware of the facts
or not being aware of the facts.

*

J.B. RHINE

Penetrating so many secrets,
We cease to believe in the Unknowable,
But there it sits nevertheless,
calmly licking its chops.

*

H.L. MENCKEN

Don't matter if you believe in them or not.
If they're there, they're there.

*

JOAN LOWERY NIXON
("THE HAUNTING")

If a man harbors any sort of fear, it makes him landlord to a ghost.

*

LORD DOUGLAS

Until we accept the fact that life itself is founded in mystery,
we shall learn nothing.

*

HENRY MILLER

I would rather live in a world where my life is surrounded by mystery,
than live in a world so small that my mind could comprehend it.

*

HARRY EMERSON FOSDICK

I allow my intuition to lead my path

*

MANUEL PUIG

Whatever the scientists may say,
if we take the supernatural out of life,
we leave only the unnatural.

*

AMELIA EDITH BARR

Uncertainties and mysteries are energies of life.

*

R.I. FITZHENRY

It is through science that we prove, but through intuition that we discover.

*

HENRI POINCARE

There must be ghosts all the world over.
They must be as countless as the grains of the sands it seems to me.
We are one and all, so pitifully afraid of the light.

*

HENRIK IBSEN

It is an unwise man who thinks what has changed is dead.

*

ANONYMOUS

Houses are not haunted.
We are haunted.

*

DEAN KOONTZ

All a skeptic is is someone who hasn't had an experience yet.

*

JASON HAWKES

A house is not haunted by spirits of people who once lived there,
but it is rather a storehouse of memories or thoughts in energy form.
When someone with an active psychic sense enters the house,
he or she can pick up these thoughts.

*

ADI-KENT THOMAS JEFFREY

One need not be a chamber to be haunted,
One need not be a house;
The brain has corridors surpassing
Material place.

*

EMILY DICKINSON

Through how many dimensions and how many media will life have to pass?
Down how many roads among the stars must man propel himself in search of
the final secret? The journey is difficult, immense, at times impossible, yet that will
not delay some of us from attempting it. We cannot know all that has happened
in the past, or the reason for all of these events, any more than we can with surety
discern what lies ahead. We have joined the caravan, you might say, at a certain
point, we will travel as far as we can, but we cannot in one lifetime see all that we
would like to see or learn all that we would hunger to know.

*

LOREN EISLEY

One thing is certain,
that nothing certain exists.

*

PLINY THE ELDER
ROMAN PHILOSOPHER 23-29 A.D.

It is better to believe than to disbelieve.
In so doing you bring everything to the realm of possibility.

*

ALBERT EINSTEIN

I don't believe that ghosts are "spirits of the dead"
because I don't believe in death...
Once you exist, you exist forever one way of another.

*

PAUL ENO

The impossible is much more closely related to reality
than the greater part of what we designate true and ordinary.
The impossible isn't perhaps the naked truth,
but I believe that it is often the truth,
undoubtedly masked and veiled, but eternal.

*

LAFCADIO HEARN

I never met a ghost I didn't like.

*

DR. HANS HOLZER

Strange to say, the luminous world is the invisible world.
The luminous world is that which we do not see.
Our eyes of flesh see only night.

*

VICTOR HUGO

We know that it (the spirit) survives the body
and that being set free from of the bars of the body,
it sees with clear gaze those things which before,
dwelling in the body, it could not see.

*

ST. AMBROSE

How difficult it is to remain just one person,
for our house is open,
there are no keys in the doors,
and invisible guests come in and out at will.

*

MARY WATKINS

Our spirit is a being of a nature quite indestructible…
it is like the sun, which seems to set to our earthly eyes,
but which, in reality, never sets but shines on unceasingly.

*

GOETHE

The body dies, but the spirit is not entombed.

*

THE DHAMMAPADA
THE BUDDHA'S PATH OF TRUTH ~ 3RD CENTURY B.C.

ABOUT THE AUTHOR

ADI-KENT THOMAS JEFFREY

Adi-Kent Thomas Jeffrey, aptly dubbed "The Mistress of the Macabre," spent a lifetime investigating psychic phenomena and the supernatural. Although she traveled the world to investigate tales of the uncanny, she always returned to her beloved Bucks County, Pennsylvania, to reflect on and write about her experiences.

A bona-fide ghost hunter, Mrs. Jeffrey chased vampires throughout Turkey and Transylvania; pursued werewolf visions in the hills of Italy; flew head-on into the "Twilight Zone" of the Atlantic Ocean called "The Bermuda Triangle" where thousands of people have disappeared without a trace; and tracked down the forbidden house of interrogation and torture maintained by the infamous Beria, head of Stalin's Secret Police during the dark reign of communism.

In 1975, she was cast into the national spotlight when her book, *The Bermuda Triangle*, was ranked #1 on the New York Times Best Seller List. Mrs. Jeffrey's other published works include over ten books recounting her mysterious experiences and discoveries.

This vibrant, dynamic and versatile woman was a frequent guest on radio and television. She appeared on *What's My Line?* and *To Tell the Truth* during the 1970s. A renowned lecturer, she spoke with knowledge and authority on the many facets of the supernatural. Mrs. Jeffrey ardently believed that truth is stranger and much more astonishing than fiction.

Her ever-popular books, *Ghosts in the Valley* and *More Ghosts in the Valley,* first published so many years ago, are classic anthologies of true and mysterious tales. Revised and expanded by the author's daughter in 2011, the updated editions of these books (along with *Haunted Village and Valley,* the final book of the trilogy) have ushered Mrs. Jeffrey's ghosts into a whole new era.

There can be no doubt that Adi-Kent Thomas Jeffrey's collections of spine-chilling stories just keep getting better with age, delighting one generation of readers after another.

GHOST TOURS OF NEW HOPE

Adele Gamble as the "Ghost of Graeme Park."

In 1981, Adi-Kent Thomas Jeffrey founded the company *Ghost Tours of New Hope*. The on-going popularity of the ghost books she had authored impelled Jeffrey to start this new business venture. It was clear that many of her readers wanted to learn more about ghostly encounters. New Hope, with its heritage of history and hauntings, served as the perfect venue for a "walk with spirits."

Mrs. Jeffrey designed an array of fascinating tours including "Ghosts 'n Gifts," "Dinner with a Ghost," "Supper and a Séance," "The Thriller Graveyard Tour" and "Haunted Village Weekend." She took great delight in introducing eager ghost hunters as well as just plain curious participants to the mysteries and the history of New

Hope, Pennsylvania.

After Jeffrey moved to Washington, D.C. in 1986, Adele Gamble took over as owner and manager of the ghost tour business. With her reverence for the world of the supernatural and her own finely tuned psychic sensibilities, Gamble has been operating the Ghost Tours of New Hope for more than twenty five years. She has received notable recognition and acclaim for her hard work, enthusiasm and successful accomplishments in marketing and expanding the business. Thanks to Adele Gamble, New Hope has become a prime destination, not only for ghost hunters, but for anyone who is eager to learn the shadowy secrets of this historic village.

For more information, please visit the website:
www.ghosttoursofnewhope.com.

*

To commemorate the 25th Anniversary of Ghost Tours, Scott Randolph produced a timeless documentary of the unearthly spirits that haunt the enchanted village of New Hope. The film, hosted by Adele Gamble, features a cast of locally talented actors reenacting some of the most fascinating stories told nightly on the tours.

Experience what it's like to spend a night in the Logan Inn's most haunted room; catch a glimpse of America's famous primitive artist, Joseph Pickett, before he vanishes into thin air; enter the "Bucket of Blood" and marvel at a kindly ghost who seeks to comfort rather than disturb.

This documentary film also includes an exclusive interview with Lynda Elizabeth Jeffrey.

Ghost Tours of New Hope DVD is available at amazon.com and arrivalvideo.com

ACKNOWLEDGMENTS

My heartfelt thanks to the countless individuals who shared their ghostly experiences with me and to the historical societies, and staff members of magazines and newspapers who aided me so graciously in this work.

Most special and profound gratitude to my husband and daughter, both precious people without whose advice and encouragement this sequel would not exist.

Adi-Kent Thomas Jeffrey   1973

More than words can say, I am thankful to Jen Rogers for her guidance, expertise, and patience, as well as the innumerable hours she spent making sure that these two books, *Ghosts in the Valley* and *More Ghosts in the Valley* would have a successful come-back.

I would also like to extend my sincere gratitude to Kreskin for the amazing job he did on writing the "Foreword" to this new book.

Many thanks to Adele Gamble who has told and re-told many of these stories to crowds of eager Ghost Tour participants for almost three decades. My mother's legacy lives on because of you.

A very special thanks is also extended to Scott Randolph and Trey Crease for their dedication to the Ghost Tours of New Hope and for their steadfast support.

A salute to Farley's Bookshop in New Hope, Pa., where my mother's ghost books first made their literary debut in the early 1970s. Farley's continued support throughout the years has been much appreciated.

Deepest love and appreciation to the host of friends who provided me with special encouragement, strength and sustenance.

Most of all, a huge thank you goes to my husband who put up with another one of my all-absorbing, time-consuming projects.

And of course, gratitude to my mother... my best, my ever friend.

Lynda Elizabeth Jeffrey   2011

CREDITS

Boonshaft, Rochelle: Illustrator
  Knocking Ghost (page 15), Ghost of Graeme Park (page 44)
Deans, Alexander: Photographer
  AKTJ at window (page 117)
Dreamstime images:
  Clock (page 9), Elm trees (page 19), Shoes (page 24), Brick church (page 51), Mining pickaxe (page 53), Victrola (page 58), Stone well (page 61), Black dove (page 67), Sea Captain (page 77), Vintage radio (page 97), Butcher knife (page 109)
IStockPhoto images:
  Voodoo bottle (page 17), Child dancing (page 22), Pirate (page 28), Lady in cap & shawl (page 30), Gibson Girl (page 31), Glass bottles (page 34), Granny (page 36), Hands in chains (page 37), Ghost bride (page 39), Deserted farmhouse (page 40), Cape May sand dunes (page 48), Hairbrush (page 55), Wolf (page 62), Sliding door (page 74), Marilyn Monroe model (page 79), Rose (page 81), Edwardian woman (page 85), Hitchhiker (page 93), Ghostly figure with candelabrum (page 96), Woman's hand (page 100), Vintage camera (page 102), Noose (page 104), Crow (page 112)
Nocella, Sam: Sunday Bulletin Staff Photographer
  Mrs. Grace Walker (page 70)
Open Clip Art Library
  Blackbeard Pirate Flag (page 29)
Pennsylvania Historical & Museum Commission
  Pennsbury Manor (page 89)
Rogers, Jennifer: Book compositor; Graphic designer; Assistant editor
Zatz, Arline: Photographer
  Author's Bio photo (page 134)

The following photographs are reproduced with the generous permission of their owners:
  Adi Alexander Thomas as an "Apparition in the Apartment" (page 65), Minnie Greenwalt and Curtis Ellsworth in "Grandmother's Ghost" (page 98), Adele Gamble as the "Ghost of Graeme Park" (page 136), AKTJ (front cover and back cover)

TRILOGY OF ADI-KENT THOMAS JEFFREY'S GHOST BOOKS

Book One: Ghosts in the Valley
An unforgettable collection of true ghost stories. This enduringly popular book includes encounters with spirits, poltergeists and phantom creatures of many kinds who once haunted and, in many cases, still haunt the homes and highways of one of America's best known areas—the Delaware Valley. To celebrate the 40th Anniversary of this book, a newly revised edition was released in 2011. With a sleek new cover, interior photographs and expanded material, the "ghosts in the valley" have never looked better!

Book Two: More Ghosts in the Valley
More fascinating tales of mysterious happenings in the Delaware Valley area. Read about authentic spooks, haunted houses, and psychic disturbances. More than 30 supernatural escapades are whimsically documented in this second volume of ghost stories. Revised and expanded by the author's daughter in 2011, this sequel offers additional proof that Adi-Kent Thomas Jeffrey will always have an enduring voice in the field of the supernatural.

Book Three: Haunted Village and Valley
Published posthumously by the author's daughter, this book offers readers one last chance to join Adi-Kent Thomas Jeffrey for a spooky walk along the dark side of the Delaware. With a special emphasis on the lingering ghosts of New Hope (including photographs), along with a section devoted to the author's own psychic experiences, this book includes 33 astonishing and authentic stories of supernatural phenomena.

ALSO

Across Our Land from Ghost to Ghost: Authentic Ghost Tales From Sea to Shining Sea
Mrs. Jeffrey shares with you more than two dozen authenticated ghost stories collected on her nation-wide search for spooks, specters, and other eerie manifestations. Read about... ghosts that haunt our nation's capitol, shadowy tales from the South, wild hauntings from the West, nerve shattering stories from the New England area, and dark encounters along the East coast.

All titles also available at amazon.com, bn.com, and at selected regional book stores.

Visit the author's websites:
www.ghostsinthevalley.com
www.hauntedvillageandvalley.com